IOWA

PAST TO PRESENT

The publisher wishes to thank the following individuals
for their help with this project:

William H. Bean
Department of Education, State of Iowa

Carol Brown
Des Moines Public Schools

Patricia Civitate
Italian-American Cultural Center, Des Moines, Iowa

Sister Jude Fitzpatrick
Superintendent of Schools, Diocese of Des Moines

Mary Lynne Jones
Des Moines Public Schools

Jonathan Levine
American Jewish Committee, Chicago, Illinois

Margaret Robinson
Des Moines Public Schools

Steffen Schmidt
*Iowa State University,
Governor's Spanish Speaking Peoples Commission, 1980–1990*

Lowell J. Soike
State Historical Society of Iowa

Dinh VanLo
Des Moines Public Schools

Photographs of nationally known Iowans, left to right: Herbert Hoover, Henry Wallace, Carrie Chapman Catt, John Atanasoff, and Grant Wood

IOWA

PAST TO PRESENT
The People and the Prairie
SECOND EDITION

DOROTHY SCHWIEDER THOMAS MORAIN LYNN NIELSEN

IOWA STATE UNIVERSITY PRESS / AMES

Dorothy Schwieder is professor of history, Iowa State University, Ames.

Thomas Morain, formerly director of research and interpretation, Living History Farms, Des Moines, is currently administrator, State Historical Society of Iowa.

Lynn Nielsen is associate professor at Malcolm Price Laboratory School, University of Northern Iowa, Cedar Fall.

Research for this book was supported by grants from the Iowa State University Achievement Foundation and the Iowa Department of Education.

The authors particularly wish to thank Jeffrey Blaga, formerly of the Malcolm Price Laboratory School, for his contributions to the project in its early stages.

Grateful acknowledgment is given to the State Historical Society of Iowa, the Historical Division of the Department of Cultural Affairs, for permission to reprint photographs from their collection. Mary Bennett gave valuable assistance in locating and selecting the photographs. Alan Schroder helped generously in the preparation of the *Teacher's Guide.*

The settlers' letters in chapter 8 first appeared in "American Letters," *The Goldfinch,* November 1981, pp. 8–9. The endorsement of the automobile in chapter 14 appeared in "The Most Satisfactory Investment for the Country Physician, Henry P. Engle, M.D., Newton, Iowa," *The Goldfinch,* November 1982, p. 6. The chart of Depression prices in chapter 17 was created for "The Cost of Living, 1934–1936," *The Goldfinch,* Fall 1978, p. 11. They are all reprinted with permission from the State Historical Society of Iowa.

Orders: 1-800-862-6657   Office: 1-515-292-0140
Fax: 1-515-292-3348   Web site: www.isupress.edu

♾ Printed on acid-free paper in the United States of America

First edition, 1989 (*through two printings*)
Second edition, 1991

Library of Congress Cataloging-in-Publication Data
Schwieder, Dorothy
    Iowa past to present : the people and the prairie / by Dorothy Schwieder, Thomas Morain, Lynn Nielsen.—2nd ed.
            p.   cm.
        Includes index.
        Summary: A textbook history of Iowa for fifth grade students.
        ISBN 0-8138-0311-X (alk. paper)
        1. Iowa—History—Juvenile literature. [1. Iowa—History.]
    I. Morain, Thomas J. II. Nielsen, Lynn. III. Title.
    F621.3.339   1991
    977.7—dc20   91-13830

Last digit is the print number: 15   14   13   12   11   10

Contents

The Study of History

The ability to tell stories makes human beings different from all other living creatures. Every nation has remembered its history by telling stories over and over. These stories tell what happened yesterday and the day before. They explain how people and places have changed and developed. But each person can tell only a small part of the tale firsthand. That is one reason why it is important to study history.

But there are other reasons, too. Sometimes we are just curious about the past. We want to know how people in other times and places dressed and traveled. We want to discover how our ancestors built homes and raised crops.

At other times we want to know what the future might bring. No one can predict exactly what will happen, and tomorrow always holds surprises. Still, we can make good guesses about the future if we know about yesterday.

Knowing about the past also helps us understand ourselves as individuals and as members of families, school groups, and clubs. For instance, each person has family stories to tell. While parts of these stories may be unique, other parts may be common to almost everyone.

People who have lived through a severe storm, a depression, or a war are part of a special group because they share a common story.

The story of Iowa includes many different chapters. It tells of American Indians planting small gardens hundreds of years ago. It relates how today's farmers harvest huge crops with modern tractors. It speaks of railroad engines puffing across the plains and swelling streams cutting through the prairies. It tells how towns started and how churches and schools developed. By understanding our state's history we learn about ourselves and our families. This is the story of Iowa.

Note to the Second Edition

This new edition includes response to teachers' comments and adds references to each chapter for further reading.

1   The Changing Land

In 1835 Lieutenant Albert Lea was traveling through eastern Iowa in search of a good location for a fort. Lea kept a journal and afterward wrote a book describing the area. *Notes on . . . the Iowa District or Black Hawk Purchase* was one of the first books about the prairies. It was also the first time that the region was called Iowa in print, and the name stuck. This is how Lea saw the area:

> The general appearance of the country is one of great beauty. It may be [seen] as one grand rolling prairie, along one side of which flows the mightiest river in the world. . . . In every part of the whole District, beautiful rivers and creeks are to be found . . . skirted by woods, often several miles in width, [giving] shelter from intense cold or heat to the animals that may there take refuge. . . . These woods also [contain] the timber necessary for building houses, fences, and boats. Though probably three-fourths of the District is without trees, yet so [well] are the water and the woods distributed throughout, that nature appears to have made an effort to arrange them in the most desirable manner possible. . . . Taking this District all in all, for [ease] of navigation, water, fuel, and timber; for richness of

soil; for beauty of appearance; and for pleasantness of climate, it surpasses any portion of the United States with which I am acquainted.

Could I present to the mind of the reader that view of this country that is now before my eyes . . . he would see the broad Mississippi with its ten thousand islands, flowing gently and lingeringly along one entire side of this District, as if in regret at leaving so delightful a region.

−Lt. Albert M. Lea, 1836

The history of Iowa is more than just the story of the people who have lived here. It is also the story of the land itself. We do not often think of the land as changing much, because in the lifetime of one person, changes are too small to notice. Yet over thousands of years, small changes make a big difference. The landscape that Albert Lea saw had taken millions of years to form. What Lea called "neat looking prairies" were once buried by mile-deep ice, and ages before the ice, Iowa had had a warm tropical climate. Throughout the state, there are fossil remains of sea creatures to prove that the whole region was once under water.

People have lived in Iowa for around twelve thousand years. That is not long compared with two billion years—the age of the oldest granite rocks found in the state. The earth as a whole is even older. Scientists believe that it has existed for almost five billion years. Picture the history of the earth as one calendar year: the first human beings appear in Iowa at two minutes before midnight on December 31.

What happened in those millions of years affects our lives today. The water we drink, the soil we farm, and the minerals we mine are there because of the way Iowa developed. Under the rich, black Iowa soil, geologists (scientists who study the history of the earth) have dis-

2

covered many layers of different kinds of rocks. Like different pages in a book, each layer tells something about the history of the land and how it was formed.

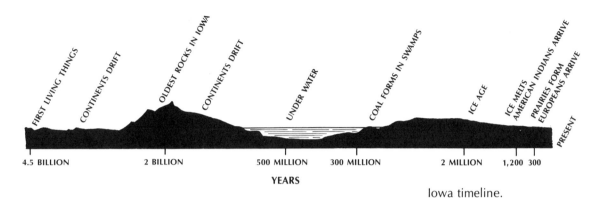

Iowa timeline.

THE LAND

Most scientists believe that four and a half billion years ago the entire earth was a ball of red-hot lava. As the surface cooled, huge sheets of solid rock formed. These sheets, called plates, floated on the molten lava beneath. Gradually, the plates carrying the continents drifted apart. Their movement was very slow, only about one inch per year, but over millions of years the continents moved into new places. Geologists think that Iowa once lay south of the equator, where it had a warm, tropical climate. From clues in its oldest rocks, they suspect that Iowa was once a mountain area, before water, winds, and ice wore it down.

Under Water

As the continents drifted apart, the oceans changed their shape. Water once covered the eastern United States. Around five hundred million years ago Iowa was at the bottom of a warm shallow sea. During that time, layers of sand, shells, and other materials collected on

Mountain to mountain rich fields roll, Ocean of soil above an ocean of stone.
—Paul Engle (Iowa poet, "Heartland," 1977)

3

the seabed. Gradually the sand formed a rock called sandstone and that layer of sandstone, deep in the earth under most of the state, is important today. Between the grains of sand are tiny spaces that can hold water. When rain falls, some of the water reaches the sandstone layer where it collects in those spaces. Many Iowa towns get their water by digging wells into the sandstone.

The limestone rock that lies under much of northeastern Iowa also comes from the bottom of the sea. Limestone makes the scenic cliffs along the Mississippi and Upper Iowa rivers. It also gives Iowa some of the greatest cave systems in the Midwest.

The Upper Iowa River carves through limestone layers, once the bottom of a sea that covered Iowa about four hundred and fifty million years ago.

State Historical Society

4

When plants and trees growing in the warm water swamps at the edge of these ancient seas died and fell, more plants grew over them. In time the sea buried the plant material under layers of mud, where slowly it changed into coal. Coal is found in southern and central Iowa, where coal mining was once a profitable industry. When railroads burned coal to make steam and homes burned coal for heat in winter, Iowans were using something that had grown three hundred million years ago.

Another product we use today comes from these ancient seas. When the water retreated and dry land appeared again, large salty lakes and bays were left. As the water dried up, the salt that was left behind turned into a rock called gypsum. Today gypsum is mined around Fort Dodge. It is used to make wallboard for building homes and offices and to make plaster and cement. Mason City cement plants use large amounts of Iowa gypsum.

In 1870 a fake giant, carved from a block of Fort Dodge gypsum, was hoisted from its "tomb." People were fooled into paying fifty cents each to view the so-called Cardiff Giant.

5

Cooling Off

Changes continued as Iowa once again became dry land. Between two and three million years ago, the climate grew colder. Scientists are not sure why. More snow fell, and much of it stayed all year. In Canada, where the climate was even colder, snow piled up and turned into huge sheets of ice. As more and more snow piled up, the ice began to push out at the edges. Roughly a million years ago, it spread out like pancake batter, completely covering the central United States. In places the glacier, as moving ice is called, was over a mile deep.

Ice covered the northern half of North America, including Iowa, several times during the Ice Age.

When the climate warmed up again, which happened from time to time, the ice melted, starting at the southern edge. But the land that reappeared was different. For one thing, it was much flatter. Ice had crushed the buried rocks into loose boulders, sand, and gravel. Glaciers carrying these rock fragments scraped the land beneath them, like sandpaper smoothing a board. The moving ice pushed hilltops into valleys and left a deep layer of sand, gravel, clay, and dust.

At the edge of the ice, glaciers dumped the last of their load in mounds and ridges. Water from the melting ice formed large lakes and rivers. Since it was too cold for growing plants to hold the soil with their roots, fierce winds picked up the loose dust and blew it back onto the ice or piled it up in hills. The loess (sounds like "bus") hills along the Missouri are some of these dust piles.

> **The ice was here, the ice was there, The ice was all around: It cracked and growled, and roared and howled . . .**
> **—Coleridge (*The Ancient Mariner,* 1798)**

State Historical Society

Dust blowing over the plains at the edge of the ice created the loess hills in western Iowa. The wind-blown soil was held in place by the tough prairie grass roots.

7

During the Ice Age the climate cooled at least four times. Each time, a new glacier scraped across the Iowa area, flattening it. Then the climate would warm up again and the ice would melt, dropping yet another layer of drift to deepen the soils of the Midwest. The last glaciation, called the Wisconsinan after the area where it has been best studied, covered only north central Iowa, moving south as far as Des Moines. When it melted, about twelve thousand years ago, it left behind flat land that would become some of the most fertile farm land in the world.

After the Wisconsinan ice retreated, the climate was cool and moist. Forests of spruce and pine trees covered most of the state. As the climate became warmer and drier, however, hardwood trees like oak, hickory, and walnut began to replace the evergreens.

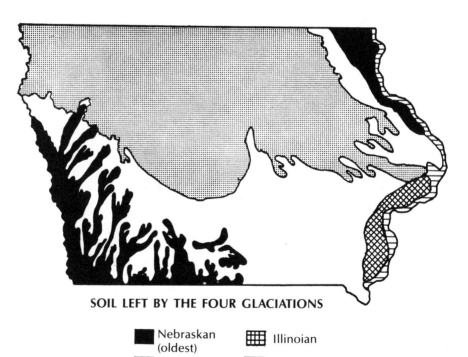

SOIL LEFT BY THE FOUR GLACIATIONS

■ Nebraskan (oldest) ⊞ Illinoian

☐ Kansan ▦ Wisconsinan (most recent)

⊟ Left by running water

Drift soils left in Iowa by each of the four great North American glaciers.

THE PRAIRIES

As the climate continued to grow warmer and less rain fell, grass appeared in patches between forests and began to spread. Summer dry spells killed many plants but not grass. When rain fell again, the roots of the grass sent up new green shoots. Gradually, areas that had once been thick forests became open grasslands. These grasslands, called prairies, spread across the northern United States, from western New York to the Rocky Mountains.

From three thousand to five thousand years ago, the climate changed again. More rain fell. What had been grasslands in the East became forests again. In Iowa, trees grew in the river valleys where they were protected from the hot dry winds.

The dots show the tallgrass prairie region at the time the settlers came.

Since then, Iowa has been a battleground. On one side are the grasses and on the other side are the trees. They compete for the soil, sunlight, and moisture that each needs to survive. If enough trees grow closely together, too little sunlight reaches the ground for grasses to grow well and the land becomes forest. On the other hand, grasses sometimes push back a forest. Thick grasses catch the falling seeds of the trees so that they never reach soil where their roots can grow. Grasses growing around the seedlings shut out the sunlight.

The grasses have a powerful partner in their war with the trees — fire. Fires used to sweep for miles across the open prairies. Started by lightning in the tall grass, prairie fires burned off everything in their path — grass, trees, and bushes. Badly burned trees do not grow again, but new grass springs up quickly from the roots safe beneath the surface. Prairie against forest, the war has gone on for centuries.

Hayden Prairie, Howard County, northeastern Iowa.

The tall prairie grass both excited and frightened the pioneer settlers. In the early 1800s (nineteenth century), soldiers and explorers traveled across Iowa and, like Albert Lea, some of them recorded their impressions of the prairie. When Lieutenant Colonel Stephen Kearney left Keokuk (in southeast Iowa) with a troop of soldiers in 1835, he wrote in his diary that the prairie grass reached his stirrups. A few days later, Kearney noted that the grass was even taller. When the men reached central Iowa, the grass was so high that the soldiers could tie it in knots over the backs of their horses.

Since Kearney and his men started their trip in June, they discovered that strawberries grew wild on the prairies. Kearney wrote in his diary that they were delicious and plentiful. The strawberries were so thick that as the horses walked through the prairie grass their hooves were stained a brilliant red. Since the men had a

The grass was so high that the soldiers could tie knots over the backs of their horses.
   —Lt. Col. Stephen Kearney (prairie expedition, 1835)

When Lieutenant Lea first saw the Iowa prairie, it was full of wildlife. There were deer and elk in the woods along the rivers and many smaller animals, such as raccoons, skunks, and foxes. Marshes and small ponds everywhere provided homes for muskrats and beavers and resting places for the huge flocks of migrating ducks and geese. These birds filled the air with their honking.

Within a short time, many things changed. Settlers plowed up the grasslands that had been home to the wildlife. They drained the ponds and wetlands to plant crops and get rid of pesky mosquitoes. As a result, there was less shelter for animals and migrating birds, which vanished from many areas of the state. People now feel sorry about the loss of wildlife and have started to preserve prairie and marsh as homes for native Iowa animals and birds.

11

cow along, they had cream and they could enjoy both strawberries and cream.

True prairies are more than just grasses, because they also include wildflowers and plants like clover. Big bluestem grass, which grows well all across the state, is one reason why the Iowa grasslands were called the tall-grass prairies. Along the edge of a marsh or with plenty of rainfall during the summer, big bluestem can grow as tall as eight or nine feet.

THE FERTILE SOIL

The prairies are important because they helped to produce the fertile soil for which the state is famous. For thousands of years, season after season, the grasses grew. Their roots filled every square inch beneath the

Feeding far countries that never have seen it, Iowa rolls onward with the rolling world.
—Paul Engle (1977)

12

soil surface. When the plants died, their roots decayed and gradually built up a rich black dirt. Soil scientists say that it takes four hundred years to produce one inch of new soil. It was this rich soil that attracted the American pioneers. They plowed up the prairies and planted corn, wheat, and oats where wildflowers and big bluestem had once grown. Corn grows well in Iowa because it too is a giant grass plant.

The settlers thought that the Iowa soil was so deep and fertile that it would last forever. But plowing it up destroyed the plants that had covered the land like a blanket. Without this cover, the land began to wash away. Rains carried dirt down the sides of hills, and rivers became muddy with topsoil.

In the 1930s, when crops withered during the long summer droughts, winds began to blow fine crumbs of soil into the air. Huge clouds of dust turned the plains into the Dust Bowl. At its worst, the dust was so thick that people turned on street lamps in daytime. Dust seeped into houses and settled on the furniture and the food on the table. On the worst days, people wore damp masks to help them breathe. Dust clouds were blown so far that ships in the Atlantic Ocean were covered with fine dust from the Midwest.

The dust storms meant that Iowa's soil was blowing away. When settlers first began plowing, there were, on average, sixteen inches of topsoil across the state. Today, there are only eight. Iowa has lost half of its most valuable resource.

> The land must be conserved with care since it is intended to be fruitful for generation upon generation.
> —Pope John Paul II (Living History Farms, 1979)

Iowa today is a product of many changes. Our climate has changed, the surface of the land was once much different, and the plants we see around us were not always here. Coal beneath the surface came from tropical

State Historical Society, Ver Steeg Collection

"A land in its working clothes" (James Hearst, "Landscape–Iowa"). Crop fields near Pella in Marion County make interesting patterns across central Iowa around 1950.

swamps. Our soil resulted from prairies growing for centuries on soil left by the glaciers.

The land affects the history of the people who live here. The most important factor in our history has been the fertile soil. Yet, without care, the soil will wash and blow away. Farmers, the government, and soil conservation groups are working to keep our soil in place. Iowa's future depends on their success.

FURTHER READING

Bonney, Margaret, ed. "Natural Resources." *The Goldfinch* 5, no. 3 (February 1984). Iowa City: State Historical Society of Iowa.

Cooper, Tom C., ed. *Iowa's Natural Heritage.* Iowa Academy of Science and the Iowa Natural Heritage Foundation, 1982.

Swaim, Ginalie, ed. "Digging into Prehistoric Iowa." *The Goldfinch* 7, no. 1 (September 1985). Iowa City: State Historical Society of Iowa.

2 American Indians

THE EARLIEST PEOPLE IN IOWA

The story of the people who have lived in what is now called Iowa goes back for thousands of years. Many different American Indian groups have hunted on the prairies and in the woodlands and planted gardens along the rivers and streams. While each tribe had its own way of doing some things, they were alike in many ways. American Indians got their food by hunting and growing food. They built shelters against the cold winters and learned the best ways to survive the changing seasons.

The state gets it name from the Ioway tribe, and many places in Iowa have taken their names from American Indians. For example, several counties are named for other Indian tribes—Sioux, Winnebago, Pottawattamie, and Sac. Others are called after Indian chiefs, like Black Hawk, Keokuk, Appanoose, and Poweshiek. The names of many Iowa rivers, cities, and towns are also Indian words.

THE EARLIEST PEOPLE IN IOWA

The very earliest people in what became Iowa left no writings to tell about themselves. Most of what we know comes from finding artifacts (things they made), such as a small piece of clay pot or a decorated shell that was part of a necklace. A pile of rocks might mark the spot of an ancient campfire.

Archaeologists, who study these artifacts, believe that human beings lived in North America for over twenty thousand years. For twelve thousand of those years there have been people in Iowa. These first "Iowans" lived in small groups and hunted large animals, such as the giant buffalo and the woolly mammoth—a sort of small elephant with shaggy brown hair. These Indian groups were nomads (people with no permanent homes), who followed the animals that supplied their food.

The earliest American Indians in Iowa hunted large game such as the woolly mammoth.

At that time, just after the ice had retreated, the Iowa climate was cooler than it is today. The winters were long and bitter, and the summers short and cool. Around nine thousand years ago, however, the climate warmed up so that more plants grew. While the early people continued to hunt large game for food and skins, they also began to gather nuts, seeds, fruits, and berries. This gave them more food than they had had in the past. About this time also, they learned how to weave fibers from plants to make cloth. In the winter, they built houses out of rocks, or shelters of brush and skins, to keep themselves warm. They also made small tools from stone and bone. One of the oldest items ever discovered in the state is a small flute made from the bone of a bird, found in northwest Iowa near the city of Cherokee.

In northeast Iowa, some Indian groups piled huge mounds of dirt into the shapes of sacred animals, such as bears, buffalo, snakes, or birds. When members of the tribe died, they were buried in the mounds.

The mound builders may have been the first to plant small gardens. At the same time, they continued to gather food from the forests. These Indians also molded pots from clay. Baking the pot for several hours in a hot

In northeast Iowa Indian mound builders piled dirt into the shape of animals. Today, some of these mounds can be seen in Effigy Mounds Park near the town of MacGregor.

fire made the clay hard enough to be used for cooking stews and storing food. Because each group had its own shapes and decorations for pots, archaeologists sometimes identify early peoples by their pottery.

Early American Indians took great care in shaping and decorating their pots, like this one from northeast Iowa. The detailed designs were often made by pressing rope into the wet clay.

State Historical Society

THE FIRST FARMERS

About a thousand years ago, new American Indian groups began moving into this area. They came up the Mississippi from the south, settled in the river valleys, and lived in large villages in the forests. In the spring, the women planted gardens of beans, squash, and corn. They were the first to discover that corn grows well in the rich Iowa soil. Some American Indian tribes regarded the garden plants as children of Mother Earth.

18

Because the women took care of the children of the tribe, they also cared for Mother Earth's children—young plants. Indian men, the hunters, were not allowed to work in the gardens.

This Winnebago woman in the 1930s tended the corn in her garden, as her ancestors had for centuries. Older women always selected the seed for the next year's planting.

State Historical Society

Corn was their most important crop. It grew first in Mexico, but as American Indians moved north up the Mississippi River, they brought corn with them. The women pounded or ground it to make cornmeal for bread, cooked it in stew pots with meat, or roasted ears at their feasts.

During the winter, the Indians lived in houses made of willow poles and elm bark, with a small hole in the roof to let the smoke escape. In their houses, they stored food, tools, and extra clothing. A tribe lived for several years on the same site. These people were not nomads. They left for the hunt but returned to the same spot each spring to plant their gardens. One tribe who lived like this was the Ioway tribe, for whom the state is named.

The home of Na-na-wa-che in the Mesquakie settlement was skillfully made from reed mats. It was the women's job to sew the mats together. Houses lasted about seven years. By then, firewood in the area would be exhausted and it was time to move on. Between six and ten people commonly lived in a house, though most activities—cooking, toolmaking, storytelling—took place outside. The house itself was used mostly for sleeping and storage.

THE TRADERS COME

In 1676, a small band of Ioway visited a French trading post at Green Bay, Wisconsin. The Ioway traded animal skins for iron kettles, glass beads, knives, and cloth—things that they could not make for themselves. In 1685, a French explorer named Nicolas Perrot visited an Ioway village on the Upper Iowa River. They held a feast in his honor, and Perrot wrote that the Ioway treated him very well.

20

The traders brought change to the Ioways' lives. The Indians acquired many items that made their lives easier. Soon they were hunting with guns rather than bows and arrows and cutting up their meat with metal knives. The women cooked stews in iron pots. They traded for colorful glass beads to decorate their new clothes of cotton cloth.

Like other tribes, the Ioway once had made everything they used. Now they came to depend on trade with the Europeans. Because the American Indians needed the skins to trade, hunting became even more important. They killed more animals than ever before to get more skins. As result, the animals became scarce and the tribes needed to find new hunting lands. This sometimes created trouble and led to battles among tribes for control of good hunting lands.

Because of these struggles, two new tribes came

When glass beads became available from European traders, Indian women became skillfull at weaving them into colorful patterns, as in this Mesquakie belt.

The Ayouwais, located about forty leagues up the river Demoin, annually consume merchandise valued at thirty-eight hundred dollars, for which they trade deer skins principally, and the skins of the black bear, beaver, otter, grey fox, raccoon, muskrat, and mink.
—North West Company agent report (1802)

[This account is based on Henry R. Schoolcraft's book on the Indian Tribes of the United States, written in 1853.]

The original outlines of the Indian map were drawn in the rough by Waw-non-que-skoon-a, an Ioway Indian, with a black-lead pencil on a large sheet of white paper at the mission house on the Ioway reservation on the Kansas-Nebraska border (16 on the map). It has been made smaller and adapted to the surveys of the public lands on the Missouri and Mississippi.

Waw-non-que-skoon-a was recording the history of the Ioways by marking the places where the tribe had lived. The marks are a symbol for a lodge, meaning a settlement. The map shows the distances that a tribe would rove. It also gives an idea of how differently the American Indians, who were hunters, used the land from the white settlers, who farmed it.

The earliest settlement in the Ioway's memory is at the junction of Rock River with the Mississippi (1). This was in or very near Winnebago territory. From this point they migrated down the Mississippi to the south fork of the river Des Moines (2). They next made an extraordinary migration, abandoning the Mississippi and its tributaries for the Missouri (3). Here they settled on a point of land formed by a small stream, called by the Indians Fish Creek. This is near Red Pipestone quarry.

They next descended the Missouri to the junction of the Nebraska, or Big Platte, River (4). They settled on the west bank, keeping the buffalo ranges on their west. Still lower down the Missouri, they next fixed themselves on the headwaters of the Little Platte River (5). From here, they returned to the Mississippi, at the mouth of Salt River (6). Here passed another period.

22

They next settled on the east bank of the Mississippi in the present area of Illinois (7). Their next migration (8) took them near their original starting point.

They moved south and west again, first to the Salt River (9) and afterwards to its source (10). They then traveled by land to the Chariton River of Missouri (11 and 12). The next two migrations were to the valley of the Grand River (13 and 14). Still continuing to the south and west, they chose the east bank of the Missouri, opposite the present site of Fort Leavenworth (15), and finally settled on the west bank of the Missouri, between the mouth of the Wolf and the Great Nemahaw, (16), where they now reside.

These migrations were probably determined by the need to find food. The Ioway relied on the deer, elk, and buffalo. As these animals moved, it is probable the Indians followed them. The Ioway stayed a dozen years at one place, on the average. This would give a period of 180 years between their arrival at their present place and 1673, when Marquette found them at the mouth of the Des Moines.

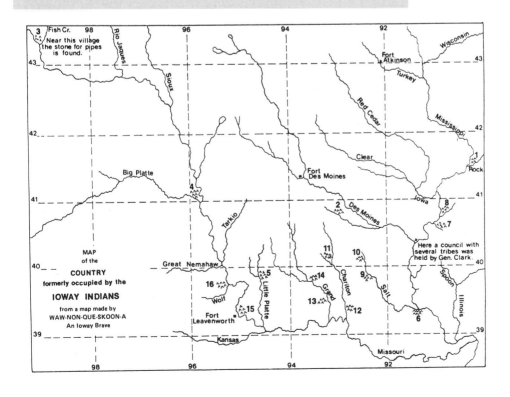

into eastern Iowa, the Sauk and the Mesquakie. The Sauk (or Sac) had once lived in northern Michigan. The Mesquakie (sometimes called Fox by the whites) were driven south from the Fox River in Wisconsin. Together, they drove away the Illinois Indians and settled along the Mississippi and Wapsipinicon rivers. From there, they controlled the hunting grounds in western Illinois and eastern Iowa.

The largest Sauk village, Saukenuk, was on the east side of the Mississippi River at the mouth of the Rock River. At one time, several thousand people lived there, fishing in the rivers and gathering nuts, berries, and fruit from the forest. The women planted large gardens of beans, pumpkins, and squash and tended hundreds of acres of corn.

Black Hawk, a Sauk chief, remembered Saukenuk as a good place to live:

> We always had plenty. Our children never cried from hunger, neither were our people in want. The rapids of Rock River furnished us with an abundance of fish, and the land being very fertile, never failed to produce good crops.

In midsummer, most of the Sauk left Saukenuk for a hunt for buffalo and elk, to the west across Iowa. When they returned, there was feasting on the meat and fresh corn from the garden. The men and boys raced horses, played games, and bartered with the traders for supplies. The women wove mats and dried food from the garden to store in deep pits for the winter.

In the late fall, the Sauk left for their winter homes. They took some food and buried the rest. When the cold weather was over, the tribe returned to Saukenuk, dug up the food stores, and began planting for the next harvest.

The Sauk tribe was divided into groups of several families called clans. Each clan had a name, like the Bear, the Thunder, or the Buffalo, and was important in religious ceremonies and other activities. A tribal council of men made important decisions. Their rules were enforced by the civil chiefs. These were the leaders of the clans, and the office was passed from father to oldest son. The tribe also had war chiefs, who led the warriors in battle. Only men who were skillful and daring fighters won that highly honored title. No one became a war chief because his father was one. When a baby boy was born, his parents marked his forehead with a small white or black dot. This meant that he belonged to one of two groups that competed with each other in games and contests of skill.

> **I liked my towns and my cornfields, and the homes of my people. I fought for it. It is now yours. Keep it as we did. It will produce good crops.**
> **—Chief Black Hawk (Fort Madison, July 4, 1838)**

TROUBLED TIMES

In 1800, the Sauk and Mesquakie were the strongest tribes along the Mississippi and the rivers that ran into it. White settlers were not allowed to move into Indian land. In fact, the United States army helped keep away pioneers.

Four years later, in 1804, the United States made a treaty (agreement) with these tribes. Five civil chiefs signed away all the land in Illinois that the tribes owned in return for gifts worth about $2,000. The government also promised to pay $600 each year to the Sauk and $400 to the Mesquakie. The tribes were allowed to remain in their homes until the land was mapped out for settlement. Then they must move west of the Mississippi. Many in the tribal council did not like the treaty. Others did not fully understand that they had sold their land. Each spring for nearly thirty years more, the Sauk returned to Saukenuk and planted their gardens.

25

White settlers, however, were moving closer. They farmed the land and cleared the forests, chasing away the animals that the Indians hunted. As a result, the native Americans had fewer skins to trade for supplies. In

CHIEF BLACK HAWK

Black Hawk, the famous war chief of the Sauk tribe, was born in 1767. He grew up in Saukenuk on the Rock River, where he earned a reputation as a daring warrior. When Black Hawk refused to leave his village in the spring of 1831, the U.S. army was called in to move him across the Mississippi to Iowa. A year later Black Hawk led 400 followers north to escape, but the army followed. Three months later the remnants of his group of men, women, and children were captured in Wisconsin, and Black Hawk was put in prison.

To convince Black Hawk that the Indians could not win, government officials took the chief east to see cities, army forts, and gun factories. He saw that fighting was useless when railroads could always bring more troops of soldiers. Everywhere on the tour, the train stations were crowded with people trying to get a glimpse of the chief. In Washington, D.C., Black Hawk met President Andrew Jackson. At that meeting the Sauk chief promised not to make war again. He was not ashamed of fighting to protect his lands. "I am a man and you are another," he told President Jackson, but he realized that there were too many whites to fight.

Black Hawk returned to Iowa to live in a small cabin with his family. During his last years, he told the story of his life to a man who wrote it down. On the Fourth of July, 1838, the chief was asked to give a speech to the citizens of Fort Madison. He was seventy-one years old.

Three months later he died. In this last speech, Black Hawk said:

The earth is our mother. We are now on it, with the Great Spirit above us. It is good.

[This is] a beautiful country. I liked my towns and my cornfields, and the homes of my people. I fought for it. It is now yours. Keep it as we did. It will produce good crops.

I thank the Great Spirit that I now am friendly with all my white brothers. We are here together. We are friends. It is His wish and mine. I thank you for your friendship.

I am now old. I have looked upon the Mississippi River. I have been a child. I love the great river. I have dwelt on its banks from the time I was an infant. I look upon it now.

State Historical Society

We always had plenty. Our children never cried from hunger, neither were our people in want.
—Chief Black Hawk (remembering Saukenuk, 1836)

1831, the government ordered the tribes to move west. The Sauk were not to return to Saukenuk anymore. Chief Keokuk advised his people that the time had come to build new villages on the Iowa side of the river.

However, the Sauk war chief, Black Hawk, refused to obey the treaty. When he led his warriors and their families back to Saukenuk the next spring, the government ordered the army to capture him. To escape from the army, some Indians fled to the north, but many were killed. Finally, Black Hawk was captured and put in prison.

To punish the Sauk and Mesquakie for the trouble Black Hawk had caused, the government made them sign a new treaty in 1832, selling even more of their land.

Keokuk, a Sauk chief, warned his people not to resist American settlement in the 1830s.

State Historical Society

This time, the United States bought land on the west side of the Mississippi in what is now eastern Iowa. It was called the Black Hawk Purchase, even though Black Hawk was in jail at the time. For this good land, the U.S. government paid the two tribes' debts and $20,000 each year for thirty years. They also promised forty barrels of salt, forty barrels of tobacco, and some blacksmithing service each year. The Indians were to leave the area by the end of June 1833.

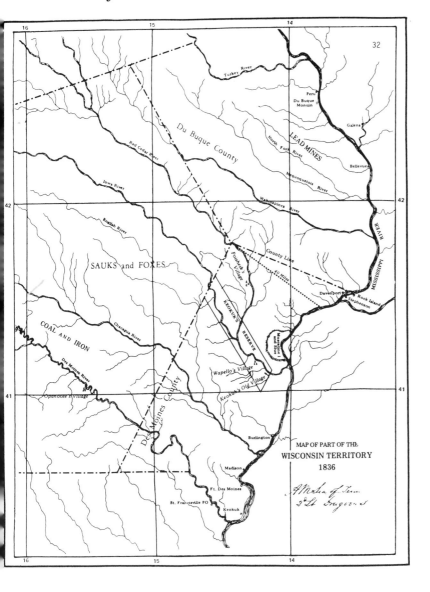

A map made by Lt. Albert M. Lea, surveyor, U.S. Dragoons, in 1836.

Government agents and traders often treated the American Indians unfairly. In 1842, the U.S. government bought another 10,000,000 acres of central Iowa for 10 cents an acre. Later the land was sold to settlers for $1.25 an acre, and the government kept the difference. The government, not the tribe, picked which Indian chief would receive the money on behalf of the tribe. These chiefs were called the "money chiefs" and had great power as long as they did what the government wanted.

Traders who sold goods to the Indians encouraged the money chiefs to buy anything they wanted for themselves. The chiefs were allowed to run up huge bills. When the payment arrived from the government, the agent paid off the money chiefs' debts first. Sometimes there was little left to distribute to the rest of the tribe. Other American Indian leaders wanted the money to go directly to the heads of Indian families. The method of payment, and the fact that they had little to say about who would speak for them, created bad feelings within the tribes.

Traders often cheated the tribes by selling them goods at sky-high prices. For example, they sold mirrors for $30 and dress coats for $60. Sometimes, they "sold" the same item twice by recording the sale twice in their record books and adding both figures to the Indians' bill.

When Iowa's new territorial governor, John Chambers, heard about this, he ordered an investigation. The traders had to return to the tribe some of the money they had overcharged for goods. After 1844, the government's annual payment to the tribe went directly to the families and the money chiefs were not allowed to distribute it. Nevertheless, the record of dealings with the Indians was not good. The government did not supervise how the money paid for the tribal lands was distributed to Indian families.

The American Indians became steadily poorer. Before long, the tribes were forced to sell even more of their land to the American government, which in turn sold it to the settlers for farms. Finally, when all their Iowa land was gone, the Sauk and Mesquakie moved to Kansas.

TRIBES IN WESTERN IOWA

Besides Sauk and Mesquakie, other tribes were pushed out of Iowa by white settlers. The Ioway had to sell their lands and move, first to Missouri and then to Kansas. Today, many Ioway live in Oklahoma. The Omaha left Ton-won-ton-ga (the big village) about twenty miles south of where Sioux City is today on the Nebraska side of the river. The Winnebago, too, were moved west to northeast Iowa and then to Nebraska.

The Sioux were the last tribe to sell their lands and leave Iowa. They lived in northern Iowa and Minnesota where they hunted on the open plains. In the fall, they harvested the wild rice that grew in the lakes. At first, the Sioux had welcomed the traders who brought blankets, guns, and tools. A Sioux chief, War Eagle, helped them choose a good spot for a trading post. (Today, Sioux City stands near the site of that post.) A trader married War Eagle's daughter.

Although they had to sell their land because they were hopelessly in debt, the Sioux did not want to leave. But finally, they left the last of their Iowa land in 1851 and moved to Minnesota and South Dakota. "Dakota" is another word for Sioux.

THE MESQUAKIE SETTLEMENT

When the Mesquakie reluctantly left Iowa, they moved to Kansas where they were homesick for Iowa. In 1856, five Mesquakie men returned to buy land where they had an earlier settlement near the town of Tama in central Iowa. Mesquakie families combined what money they had and sold some of their ponies. Together they bought eighty acres of land. With the permission of the Iowa governor, seventy-six Mesquakie returned to Iowa to settle on the land they now owned. A few Mesquakie had never gone to Kansas but had continued to live along the rivers of eastern Iowa. These scattered groups joined the rest on the land near Tama.

Mesquakie Indians keep alive their traditional dances at their annual summer powwow near Tama.

State Historical Society

The Mesquakie land in Iowa is called a settlement. It is not a reservation. The government holds a reservation for the Indian people who own it but do not have control. The Mesquakie own the land together, which means that no family owns any part by itself. Decisions about the settlement are made in a tribal council elected by the Mesquakie. The tribe has had to make difficult decisions, such as whether to become more like whites or to continue their Indian traditions. Because their land is too small for much hunting, the men have had to learn new ways to make a living.

Today, the Mesquakie still live on their settlement. Their children attend school on the settlement and in Tama, and some go on to college. Every year, the tribe hosts a summer powwow where they dance traditional dances and display their crafts. This is like a homecoming for the Indian people, and visitors attend to learn more about their American Indian neighbors. Through their settlement, education programs, and tribal councils, the Mesquakie keep many of their traditions alive.

Iowa's history begins with the American Indians who lived here for thousands of years, hunting, gathering, and growing their food and supplies. That way of life changed when the European traders came. The Indians no longer had to make everything they needed. Then settlers wanted the land for farming. Before long, most of the American Indian tribes were pushed out of Iowa.

Today only the Mesquakie of Tama County live together on their own land, although Indian families from several tribes live in many Iowa towns, especially Des Moines and Sioux City. Some have given up their Indian traditions, but others still practice tribal customs.

FURTHER READING

Anderson, Duane, *Eastern Iowa Prehistory.* Ames: Iowa State University Press, 1981.
Bonney, Margaret, ed. "Indians of Iowa." *The Goldfinch* 3, no. 4 (April 1982). Iowa City: State Historical Society of Iowa.
Vogel, Virgil J. *Iowa Place Names of Indian Origin.* Ames: Iowa State University Press, 1983.

3 Many Flags over Iowa

any streams flow together to make Iowa history. One is the history of the American Indian people who have lived in the region for thousands of years. Another is the story of explorers and settlers from Europe and their descendants whose stay in Iowa has been shorter. The first Europeans came only about three hundred years ago. Iowa's latest settlers came from Southeast Asia as refugees in the 1970s and 1980s. They were invited by the governor of Iowa so they could escape political persecution and physical harm due to civil war in their own countries.

Just as there were different tribes of American Indians with their own customs and languages, there were also different groups of Europeans. Both the French and the English wanted to build an empire in North America. The outcome of that struggle was important for the future of Iowa.

THE FRENCH

The French were the first to explore the land that became Iowa. In 1673, seven men, led by Louis Jolliet,

34

pushed their canoes onto the Great Lakes. Father Marquette, a Catholic priest, kept a journal of the expedition. Leaving the French settlements in eastern Canada, on the St. Lawrence River, they set out across the Great Lakes. At what is today Green Bay, Wisconsin, the men left Lake Michigan and paddled up the Fox River. From the Indians, they learned how to reach another river that would carry them west. They carried their canoes "2,700 paces" across land, according to Father Marquette, to the Wisconsin River where they reloaded and set out again.

On June 17, they reached the mouth of the Wisconsin River where it flows into a great river heading south, the Mississippi. The French were very impressed with the beauty of the land. Across the river were high bluffs covered with heavy forests. It was at this spot, near the present town of McGregor, that Europeans first saw what is now Iowa.

The French explorers went ashore farther down the

> **At first, when we were told of these treeless lands, I imagined that it was a country ravaged by fire, where the soil was so poor that it could produce nothing.**
> **—Father Marquette (French missionary explorer, 1673)**

Jolliet and Marquette first reached Iowa where the Wisconsin River flows into the Mississippi. Today this historic site is Pike's Peak State Park.

river and met some Indians of the Illinois tribe camped there. With the arrival of these explorers, Indian history and European history began to flow together like those two rivers.

As the explorers continued their trip down the Mississippi, they sometimes saw the treeless prairies stretching down nearly to the river's edge. The prairies made a deep impression on Marquette, who wrote in his journal:

> At first, when we were told of these treeless lands, I imagined that it was a country ravaged by fire, where the soil was so poor that it could produce nothing. But we have certainly observed the contrary; and no better soil can be found, either for corn, or for vines, or for any other fruit whatever.

Jolliet and his men sailed down as far south as the Arkansas River. By then, they were certain that the Mississippi flows into the Gulf of Mexico and not the Pacific Ocean as some had predicted. They turned around and paddled back to Canada to report on their mission.

Nine years later, another French explorer named La Salle sailed all the way from the Great Lakes to the Gulf of Mexico. At the mouth of the Mississippi River, he raised a French flag and claimed for France all lands drained by that river. La Salle called the region Louisiana in honor of the French king, Louis XIV. Louisiana included all the land from the Rocky Mountains to the Appalachian Mountains and from the Great Lakes to the Gulf of Mexico.

Claiming this huge area for France did not mean that the French wanted to live there. A claim told other European nations to stay away. It declared that France would try to prevent settlers from other European coun-

The first European to settle in Iowa was Julien Dubuque. He was born in Canada in 1762. Early records describe him as a short man with black hair and black eyes.

When he was in his early twenties, Dubuque traveled to Prairie du Chien, an important trading post on the Mississippi River in what is today Wisconsin. There, he learned that there were rich deposits of lead across the river in Iowa, on lands held by the Mesquakie Indians. Lead was a valuable metal because it was used to make "shot" (used in guns). Dubuque gave the Mesquakies many presents and learned their language. Finally, they agreed to allow him to mine the lead on their land. He was the only European given this right.

Women and old men from the Mesquakie tribe dug the lead ore from the ground. Dubuque and his French Canadian helpers melted it down and poured it into bars called "pigs," which were shipped down the Mississippi River and sold in St. Louis. He also shipped loads of furs that the Mesquakies had traded for goods from St. Louis. He became a well-known and popular trader in St. Louis.

When the king of Spain claimed the land on the west side of the Mississippi River, Dubuque named his lead works "The Mines of Spain." This flattered the Spanish governor, who granted Dubuque ownership of a large area of land along the river.

Later, Dubuque fell into debt and had to give up his business. He died a poor man, but the Mesquakie still considered him to be a friend. The city of Dubuque was named after him.

Lead mining continued to be an important industry in the area for many years. Some of the lead was made directly into shot. Lead was melted in large kettles at the top of a tall stone shot tower. Then drops of hot liquid lead were dripped from the top of the tower. The drops cooled as they fell. When they reached the ground, they were hard and round. Workers collected them and shipped them out in barrels or crates.

tries from living there or trading with the Indians of the region. Fur trading was the chief industry of the French in North America. Though claims became important later, they meant little at first to the daily lives of the American Indians.

THE ENGLISH

The English did not agree with the French claim. They also claimed the land and planned to build settlements on it. The English had established colonies along the Atlantic Coast from Canada to Georgia. At first, the Appalachian Mountains made it hard for the English to move west.

In 1756, the English and French went to war over their claims in North America. By the end of the war, the English had gained control over most of the land once held by the French. Although there were no European settlers in Iowa at the time, the English victory was important for Iowa history. It meant that French people would not control the future of the region.

THE SPANISH

Knowing that the English were winning, the French secretly gave their claim to Spain. They wanted to keep the lands west of the Mississippi, including Iowa, from falling under English control. England, however, soon had other problems. In 1776, the American colonies declared their independence and, by winning the American Revolution, became an independent nation. The treaty that ended the fighting set boundaries for the new United States. The Mississippi River was the western edge of the new nation. This meant that Iowa was not part of the original United States. The land west of the river, including Iowa, was still claimed by Spain. Hispanic Iowans today remember Spain's early role in their state's history.

THE LOUISIANA PURCHASE

Ten years after the American Revolution, a new leader came to power in France. Napoleon led French armies to victories and dreamed of rebuilding a French empire in North America. He forced Spain to return Louisiana to France in 1800 and began making plans to send French settlers there.

To the United States, the land west of the Missis-

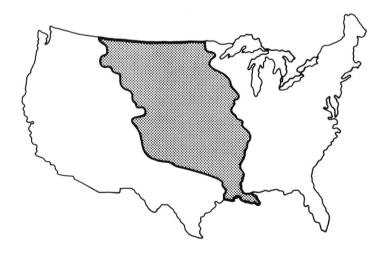

The map shows the land in the Louisiana Purchase. In 1803, America wanted to buy a city (New Orleans). Instead, France sold them an empire for a price that worked out to be less than three cents per acre. It was the greatest land bargain in U.S. history.

39

When the American diplomats arrived, Napoleon wanted to sell New Orleans— and all of Louisiana —for fifteen million dollars.

sippi River was not nearly as important as the river itself. American farmers living west of the Appalachian Mountains shipped farm products on river barges and flatboats. All rivers flowed into the Mississippi and down to the port of New Orleans. President Thomas Jefferson feared that Napoleon might some day forbid Americans to use the Mississippi for shipping. If Napoleon closed New Orleans to American riverboats, American farmers would be hurt.

To prevent this, President Jefferson sent two diplomats to France with an offer to buy Florida and the city of New Orleans for up to ten million dollars. In the meantime Napoleon had decided not to rebuild a French empire in North America. When the American diplomats arrived, Napoleon wanted to sell New Orleans—and all of Louisiana—for fifteen million dollars. The diplomats recognized this as a great bargain for the United States and accepted the offer. When the treaty for the Louisiana Purchase was signed in 1803, the size of the United States doubled. The new nation now spread from the Rocky Mountains to the Atlantic Ocean, and the future Iowa had become part of the United States.

THE AMERICANS

For many years, President Jefferson had been interested in learning about the western lands. Even before they had been purchased from France, Jefferson had organized a secret exploration party headed by his friend, Captain Meriwether Lewis. Lewis picked as his assistant, Lieutenant William Clark.

In 1804, Lewis and Clark set out to find what America had bought for its fifteen million dollars. The crew left St. Louis to find the source of the Missouri

40

River. They were instructed to report on Indian tribes in the area, the best places for future trading posts and forts, and the nature of the country. As they poled their boats up the Missouri River, they passed along Iowa's western border. There the river winds back and forth, and their progress was slow. They traveled for months to the headwaters of the Missouri River, left their boats, and crossed the Rocky Mountains to the Pacific Ocean. Returning down the Missouri, the crews arrived in St. Louis in 1806 to a great celebration. Their reports on their trip greatly increased the information about the new territory.

Another American explorer, Zebulon Pike, set out to learn more about the Mississippi River. In 1805, he left St. Louis and pushed up the river. He explored both sides of the river and recommended several places for forts and trading posts.

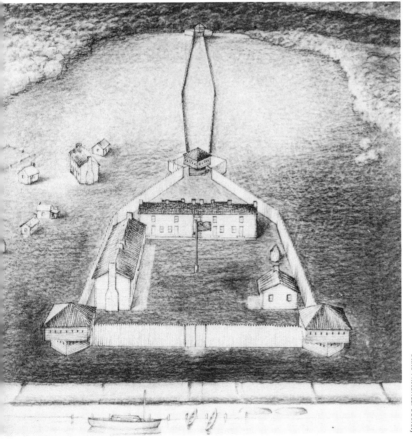

Fort Madison on the Mississippi River was built in 1808 to impress the Indians and help the fur trade. The square buildings on the corners allowed soldiers to fire down on attackers who tried to scale the walls.

State Historical Society

> No better soil can be found, either for corn, or for vines, or for any other fruit whatever.
> —Father Marquette (1673)

Unfortunately, the army did not build a fort where Pike suggested. Instead, it built Fort Madison. In 1812, when the United States was again at war with England, the English urged American Indians to attack Fort Madison. Then the army discovered that the location of the fort made it hard to defend. The soldiers dug a ditch to the river at night and sneaked to their boats. They set fire to the fort as they left and paddled down the river in the dark.

EXPLORING THE PRAIRIES

While trees grew along the rivers, most of Iowa was covered with tall grasses. The prairies were a new experience for settlers. The eastern lands had been forested, but in Iowa, one could travel through tallgrass prairies for miles and hardly even see a tree.

Some early explorers thought the prairies were beautiful. They described the way the wind made the tall grass sway back and forth like waves of the sea. They marveled at the beautiful prairie flowers that splashed the open fields with color. Others disliked the prairies. Zebulon Pike described some of the western prairies as "a desert." Another early visitor to a winter prairie wrote that "a prospect more bleak and lonely" was impossible to imagine. These people missed the trees. For them, the prairie was too open and flat.

> The prairies are miserably poor and will not have a single bush on them for ages.
> —James Monroe (1806)

At first many thought that the soil on the prairies must not be fertile because no trees grew there. They judged how rich the soil was by what grew on it—a land that could not even grow trees must be poor indeed. James Monroe, who later became president of the United States, once described the prairies as "miserably poor" and predicted that they "will not have a single bush on them for ages." Others, like Lieutenant Albert Lea, disagreed and reported that the soil was rich.

As the government opened parts of Iowa to American settlers, those who had described it as a barren wasteland were proved wrong. The land was incredibly fertile, and news of the rich soil spread rapidly. Pioneers loaded their wagons and headed to the "land across the river." In 1836, there were about 10,500 American settlers in Iowa. Ten years later, there were 96,000. Most had come to farm the rich soil.

Iowa had been the land of the American Indians, the French, the Spanish, and the Americans. In 1800, the area was claimed by France and occupied by Indian tribes. Fifty years later, it was part of the United States with a growing population. People from all over the world were coming to settle on the prairies. Things might have been different, of course. What if France had defeated England and French colonists had settled the Mississippi valley? What if the English colonists had not won their independence but remained part of the British empire? Events happening many miles away, even on another continent, have influenced Iowa's history and will influence its future.

FURTHER READING

Sage, Leland L. "Iowaland: Indian, French, Spanish, American, 1673–1803." In *A History of Iowa*. Ames: Iowa State University Press, 1974. Chapter 2.

Swaim, Ginalie, ed. "The Fur Trade." *The Goldfinch* 6, no. 2 (December 1984). Iowa City: State Historical Society of Iowa.

Wall, Joseph F. "We Occupy the Land and Organize It." In *Iowa: A Bicentennial History*. New York: W. W. Norton, 1978. Chapter 2.

Pioneers on the Prairie

In the nineteenth century, thousands of people left the East to establish new homes in the West. At first they settled in states like Ohio and Indiana, but by the 1830s settlers were moving into Iowa. Soon after their arrival, the newcomers wrote letters to friends and relatives back East telling them about Iowa's fertile soil. Between 1833 and 1870, almost one million people came to live in Iowa. By 1870, most of the state had been settled and farms and small towns had appeared everywhere.

THE EARLY SETTLERS

Most of the people who settled in Iowa before the Civil War (1861–1865) came from the northeastern United States and the states of Ohio and Indiana. Some Southerners also migrated to Iowa in the 1840s and 1850s, mostly from Kentucky, Virginia, and Missouri. Along with settlers from the Northeast and the South, many Europeans immigrated to Iowa. (Immigrants are people born in a different country who move to the United States.) Although more came from Germany than any other foreign land, people also came from Holland, the British Isles, and the Scandinavian countries. Most immigrants came to Iowa because they knew they could buy good land for little money.

Birthplace of native-born residents of Iowa: Census of 1870

Total state population: 1,194,020
Total native-born population: 989,328

Connecticut	5,185	New Jersey	5,688
Illinois	65,391	New York	79,143
Indiana	64,083	North Carolina	5,090
Iowa	428,620	Ohio	126,285
Kentucky	14,186	Pennsylvania	73,435
Maine	5,943	Tennessee	6,085
Maryland	5,972	Vermont	12,204
Massachusetts	8,929	Virginia and West Virginia	19,563
Michigan	8,918	Wisconsin	24,309
Minnesota	2,683	Other states and	
Missouri	13,831	territories	7,728
New Hampshire	5,057		

Birthplace of foreign-born residents of Iowa: Census of 1870

Total state population: 1,194,020
Total foreign-born population: 204,692

Austria	2,691	Holland	4,513
Bohemia	6,765	Ireland	40,124
British America	17,907	Norway	17,554
Denmark	2,827	Sweden	10,796
France	3,130	Switzerland	3,937
Germany	66,162	Other European, African,	
Great Britain	25,318	and Asian countries	2,967

Once people decided to come to Iowa, it took them a long time to get here. In the 1840s and 1850s, people traveled from Ohio and Pennsylvania by covered wagon. Later on, others were able to take the railroad for part of the way. One family bound for Iowa, Hosea and Mary Ann Newton, left their home in Connecticut in 1858. First they traveled on a stagecoach, then a steamboat, and finally on a railroad to Louisa County where the railroad ended. For the last leg of their journey, the Newtons hired a man and his team of horses to take them to their new home in Keokuk. Families often walked the last part of their journey.

Route taken by the Fairchild family.

Ephraim Fairchild moved to Iowa with his wife and children in 1857. Helped by an uncle, Jeremiah Gard, who owned land nearby, the Fairchilds settled on a farm in Jones County. This letter describes the journey west from their home in New Jersey to Jones County, Iowa.

Pleasant Ridge, March 23, 1857
Ever Kind and affectionate Father and Mother and all the rest of the friends. I take my pen in hand to write a few lines to you to let you know that we are all well at present and hope these few lines may find youall the same.

I will try to tell you some thing aboute our journey oute west. we had a very slow trip, the carrs run verry slow all the way from Jersey City up to Dunkirk [N.Y.] so we did not make connection with the train from their and had to stop there from 2 oclock in the afternoon until 2½ oclock wednesday morning. then we Started for cleveland and arrived there aboute noon and missed the train there again. we had to stay their till about 4 oclock in the evening. then we started for toledo and there we made connection with the wagon [train] going to chicago and there we had to stop about 4 or 5 hours longer. then we started about 9 in the evening for Dunleath [now called East Dubuque]. we arrived there about 9 or 10 on friday morning and there we met uncle Jerry. he started from home on wednesday and arrived at Dubuque on thursday and on friday we crossed the missippia on the ice with the horses and wagon. then we started for uncle Jerrie's.

we got as far as the 11 mild [mile] house. then we put up and in the morning we started again and went about 1 mild and broke the arm of the axel tree. then we was in a fix. no house nearer than a mild but Eliza and the children got out of the wagon and went on to the 12 mild house afoot and uncle and I unloded the things into another wagon and fixed up the wagon so as to get to the 12 mild house and there was a black smith shop and the smith thought he could fix it. so he went at it as soon as he cood and when he got it fixed it was about 2 or 3 oclock. then we started again and traveled on until night. then we put up at Ozark with a man by the name of E. West. They were verry nice people. the next morning which was sunday morning it thundred and lightened and rained quite hard untill about 9 oclock, then it stopped and about 10 uncle said he thought we had better start before the river at canton got so high that it wood be dangerous. so we started and got acrost the river safe and went on home, we got to uncles about 4 oclock sunday after noon all safe and sound but mudier going I never saw in my life.

                                        – Ephraim G. Fairchild

When European immigrants came to the United States, they traveled on either sailing ships or steamships. Families might board a ship in Bristol, England, or Amsterdam, Holland, to make the trip to America. Sometimes it took a boat six weeks to cross the Atlantic Ocean. The voyage was so long and difficult that people often became sick. Many immigrants landed in New Orleans where they boarded steamboats to travel up the Mississippi River. About three weeks later, they arrived in one of Iowa's river cities.

People coming to Iowa in the 1800s mostly came in family units. The newcomers would bring along their children and maybe their parents, too. Sometimes two brothers and their wives and children traveled together, building their farms side by side on the Iowa prairie. It was the practice for families to help each other find land and build their homes.

WOODLAND AND PRAIRIE

When people arrived in Iowa in the 1830s and 1840s, most of them viewed the prairie for the first time. For many, it seemed strange and unpleasant because most of the newcomers came from states where trees were plentiful. In the early 1800s the northeastern United States had so many trees that it was said that a gray squirrel could jump from tree to tree for seven hundred miles and never touch the ground.

Because of the abundance of timber, people in the Northeast used wood for all their needs. In their log cabins, they burned wood for fuel and for light in the evenings. They ate on wooden tables, rocked their babies in wooden cradles, and served their soup with wooden ladles. Farmers also built fences from wood. These people had developed a woodcraft for their lifestyle.

48

A split-rail fence showing the corner connection.

Once settlers arrived in Iowa, however, they could no longer practice woodcraft. In extreme eastern Iowa, the firstcomers found enough timber to build log cabins and fill their other needs. But those who came next had to travel farther into Iowa to find land. They settled on the prairie, which was covered with tall grass but lacked trees.

Like Lieutenant Lea, many of Iowa's new settlers were excited about the beauty of the prairie. They delighted in the wildflowers that bloomed through the summer. During June, yellow, white, and pink flowers were everywhere. By July, the wood lilies were in bloom, and in late summer, yellow coneflowers and goldenrod covered the prairie. Throughout the summer, the land was a brilliant carpet of pink, red, purple, yellow, and orange.

Not all settlers thought the prairie was inviting. Some were homesick because Iowa looked so different from their homes back East. One woman from New York told her husband that she thought she would die because there were no trees near her new home. Immigrants from the Scandinavian countries felt particularly strange on the prairie. They missed the valleys and tree-covered mountains in their native lands.

Once settlers had moved onto the grassland, they had to find substitutes for wood. There were usually enough trees along rivers and streams to build log cabins, but pioneers had to experiment with different materials for fuel and fencing. In an attempt to build fences, some settlers stacked rocks into walls. Others planted hedges and discovered that the fast-growing Osage orange made the thickest fence.

For fuel, families sometimes burned dried prairie grass, which they had tied into tight knots. In one hour, two children could tie enough hay knots to provide fuel for an entire day. Other families burned corncobs or cow chips (dried cow manure). Settlers living in southern Iowa soon discovered that coal jutting out from riverbanks and ravines made a good fire.

In the 1870s, pioneers began moving into extreme northwest Iowa where there were almost no trees. These families faced the greatest adjustment to the prairie environment. Again they experimented with different materials, using sod (clumps of earth with grass and roots) to make homes. Once built, a sod house provided a good, warm place to live. When winter winds howled across the prairie, the sod houses stood firm, held solidly in place by the weight of the dirt itself.

In addition to a lack of timber, Iowa's early settlers faced the problem of prairie fires. In the fall, lightning or any spark could start a blaze raging in the dry grass. Prairie fires were frightening because they burned so rapidly. Once a fire was spotted, every man, woman, and child was expected to help beat it out. At night, a prairie fire was a spectacular sight, with flames sometimes rising thirty feet into the air.

John and Sarah Kenyon moved to Delaware County, Iowa, from Rhode Island in 1856. John and Sarah rented land from her father, Richard Ellis. In this letter John Kenyon describes their fight to save their lives and property from an approaching prairie fire.

Monday eve Oct 23d

. . . and now for the prarie fire we had a week ago yesterday. I went to window and looked out and it was about 1½ miles of[f]. I could [see] nothing but smoke and it looked awful dark. I grabed the hoe and scythe and started for our south road about 20 rods from the house, when I got there the fire had just reached the road. it come in the shape of a V and the flames roled higher [than] the waves on the ocean. it looked awfull to me. I was so frightened that I shook like a dog. . . . it had crossed the road. I run for life and put it out and followed it up the road ten rods or so untill it was past our land. I hurried back but it had crossed the road in another place and was within ten feet of the fence. Father Ellis and Mother and Ann was fighting of it like mad (as the english say) with foot mats rag rugs old pieces of carpet coats and petticoats &c. we fought it to the corn field then it had to side burn about 20 rods then it had a clean sweep for the hay. stables and house chicken coops hogs sties all made of hay and poles but the house. Father and me stayed and fought it and the women folks cut it for the stacks and raked

> It come in the shape of a V and the flames roled higher [than] the waves on the ocean.
>
> —John Kenyon (pioneer, Delaware County, 1859)

51

up all the old stalks they could. Mary she come just as the fire was comeing round the fields. she grabed bed close of [clothes off] the bed carpeting any thing she could lay her hands on. . . . had all wet ready for action, on came the fire and how they kept it of[f] the stock the Lord only knows. I was [so] frightened that I dare not look that way. if it had not [been] for the female department everything would burn. they fought like heroes. Beaches and Joneses folks had almost as narrow escape as we but not quite so long. they had it about an hour and we 4 or 5 hours. they said they fought so hard they would come out of the fire and smoke and throw them selfs on the ground. they thought they was going up. I did not fight hard as that but I fought hard enoughf to burn of[f] my whiskers and hair so I had to have them cut. I looked rather red around the jaws . . .

— John B. Kenyon

SURVEYING AND PURCHASING LAND

Once families had arrived in Iowa, the first thing they needed to do was to buy land. But before they could do that, the federal government had to survey (measure and map) the land. The survey marked out townships, which were six miles square and contained thirty-six sections. In turn, each section contained 640 acres (an acre is about the size of a football field) and each acre contained 43,560 square feet. The surveys were done by men hired by the federal government and it took twenty-three years to survey what is now the state of Iowa.

After an area had been surveyed, the government set up a land office where people could buy land. Officials announced a date for a land auction and advertised the

52

sale in nearby newspapers. The day of the sale, an agent auctioned off a few acres at a time. Most settlers bought eighty acres. Since they usually paid $1.25 an acre, that meant that they paid $100 for their land. Today $100 sounds like a very small amount of money for a farm, but in the 1830s and 1840s, many families did not have more than a few dollars. Some families had to work several years before they could save $100.

6	5	4	3	2	1
7	8	9	10	11	12
18	17	16*	15	14	13
19	20	21	22	23	24
30	29	28	27	26	25
31	32	33	34	35	36

Diagram of a township.

*Reserved for education

Section 31

Lots

NW Quarter		1	2	3	4
NW Quarter		South half NE Quarter			
West half of SW Quarter	NE 4 of SW 4	SE Quarter			
West half of SW Quarter	SE 4 of SW 4	SE Quarter			

In pursuance of law, I, John Tyler, President of the United States of America, do hereby declare and make known, that public sales will be held at the undermentioned land offices in the Territory of Iowa, at the periods hereinafter designated to wit:

At the Land Office at FAIRFIELD (late Burlington) commencing on Monday, the sixth day of February next, for the disposal of the public lands within the limits of the undermentioned townships, to wit:

North of the base line, and West of the fifth principal meridian.

Township seventy-seven, of range six.

Townships seventy-six and seventy-seven, of range seven.

Townships seventy-four, seventy-five, seventy-six, and seventy-seven of range eight.

Townships seventy-two, seventy-three, seventy-four, seventy-five, and seventy-seven of range nine.

Townships seventy, seventy-one, seventy-two, and seventy-three, of range ten.

Township sixty-nine, of range eleven.

At the Land Office at DU BUQUE, commencing on Monday, the twentieth day of February next, for the disposal of the public lands within the limits of the undermentioned townships, viz:

North of the base line, and West of the fifth principal meridian.

Townships eighty, eighty-one, eighty-two, and eighty-three, of range five.

Townships seventy-eight, eighty, eighty-one, eighty-two, eighty-three, eighty-four, and eighty-five, of range six.

Townships seventy-eight, to eighty-seven, inclusive, of range seven.

Lands appropriate by law for the use of schools, military, or other purposes, will be excluded from sale.

The sales will each be kept open for two weeks, (unless the lands are sooner disposed of,) and no longer, and no private entries of land in the townships so offered, will be admitted until after the expiration of the two weeks.

Given under my hand, at the city of Washington, this twenty-seventh day of September, Anno Domini, 1842.

By the President   John Tyler

Tho. H. Blake,
Commissioner of the General Land Office.
(Burlington) *Iowa Territorial Gazette and Advertiser,*
November 5, 1842.

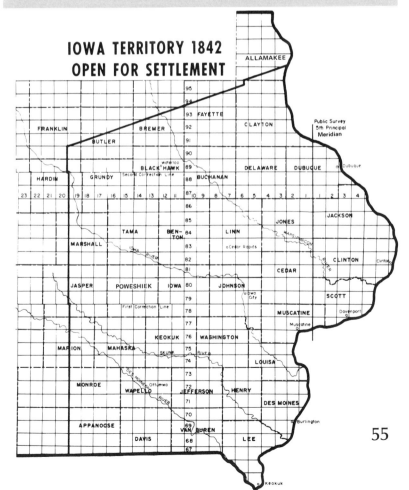

IOWA TERRITORY 1842
OPEN FOR SETTLEMENT

55

At the end of the auction, a government clerk listed each land sale in a book that was later sent to Washington, D.C., for safekeeping. Each person who bought land received a deed that stated exactly what piece of land had been purchased. Because of this careful system, there were few disagreements over land boundaries.

As well as buying land from the government, people could obtain land other ways. The earliest settlers often took advantage of squatters' rights. Squatters claimed land by settling on it and making their own boundaries. In most parts of Iowa the surveys were finished before the settlers arrived, but in southeastern Iowa, squatters arrived first. They usually just "walked off" what they thought would be about eighty acres of land. Sometimes they had walked off the right amount of land and sometimes they had not. Later when the surveys were done, squatters had to bring their boundaries in line with those of the official surveyors.

Another way to get land was from the railroads. The federal government gave land to railroads to encourage them to build lines into the central part of the country. The railroads, in turn, sold most of this land to settlers in order to raise money to build more lines. In Iowa, people bought land from the Illinois Central, the Chicago and North Western, the Rock Island, and the Burlington railroads. People often paid $8 or $10 for an acre of railroad land.

Some people coming into Iowa got their land by serving in the army. Beginning early in our history, the government used land in an interesting way. Because there was little money to pay soldiers, the government sometimes used land as an attraction for joining the army. It promised that if the men joined the army they would receive a piece of land when they finished their term. The government followed this practice for many years. Men serving in the Black Hawk War (1832) and the Civil War were sometimes paid with 120 acres of land in Iowa.

Most of the early settlers came to Iowa from other places in the United States, although some arrived from Europe. The journey was slow and difficult in the 1840s and 1850s, before railroads were built all the way to Iowa. Many families walked the last part of the way. For newcomers, the biggest change was learning how to live without plentiful timber. Their greatest fear was a prairie fire raging across the dry grasslands.

Pioneers came because they wanted cheap land. Some bought it from the railroads, some had army grants, and some squatters just moved in and made a claim. But the greatest number bought their land from the government. Before the federal government sold land in Iowa, the area was surveyed and marked out in township squares of six miles on each side. Each township was divided into thirty-six sections and each section into quarter sections of 160 acres. This careful system prevented quarrels over land boundaries.

FURTHER READING

Fairchild, Ephraim G. Collection, March 1857–October 1858. Manuscript Collection. Iowa City: State Historical Society of Iowa.

Kenyon, John B., and Sarah Kenyon Collection, August 29, 1856–March 2, 1865, Manuscript Collection. Iowa City: State Historical Society of Iowa.

Swaim, Ginalie, ed. "Life on the Iowa Prairies." *The Goldfinch* 7, no. 2 (November 1985). Iowa City: State Historical Society of Iowa.

5

Pioneer Life on the Prairie

The first job for the earliest settlers on the Iowa prairie was to build a house. If there was enough wood, they would build a log cabin. Otherwise, they learned how to make a snug sod house. There were few stores where pioneers could buy supplies, so families had to make or grow almost everything they needed. First the pioneers had to break the prairie sod. Then they planted crops to feed the animals that fed the family. Later on, they raised extra crops and animals for sale. Although pioneer life in Iowa was hard, it was not lonely. Farms were close together and a good deal of visiting went on.

BUILDING HOMES ON THE PRAIRIE

Once pioneers had land, the next task was to build a house. In Iowa, most early settlers built small log cabins that measured around sixteen by eighteen feet. The cabins usually had one room with an overhead loft where the children slept during warm weather. When it turned cold, children slept on straw pallets in front of the fire.

58

The fireplace was the chief feature in the cabin. In winter, it provided heat for the family and at night it gave light. Most important, the fireplace was the place for cooking food.

Pioneer cabins were crowded. Most families had at least three or four children and everyone had to live in one or two rooms. With so many people, there was little space for furniture. Most cabins contained at least one bed, a small cupboard, a table, and a few chairs or stools. Pioneer women usually had a spinning wheel and a loom that they set up when they needed to weave cloth.

During Iowa's cold winters, life was especially difficult. Often it was hard to stay warm. Sometimes in bitterly cold weather families went to bed because that was the only way they could keep from getting badly chilled or even frostbitten. In the first years of settlement, some cabins did not have wooden floors, so the owners had to stand on the frozen ground. Sometimes pioneer women stood on a block of wood to do their work.

> **Select 60 to 80 tall and straight trees.**
> *—1870 Iowa State Almanac ("How to Build a Log Cabin")*

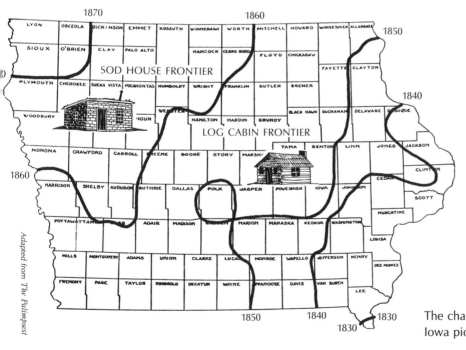

Adapted from The Palimpsest

The changing frontier of the Iowa pioneers.

59

Building a log cabin is a difficult task. It is a good idea to invite friends and neighbors to help with the felling, notching, and raising of the logs. It can be a social event. Some of the homesteaders provide not only food, but also buy a keg of liquor. This seems to make the work easier.

In planning your log cabin, choose a sheltered spot. Protection from the north wind will enable you to keep a warmer cabin during Iowa's severe winters. After picking a site, level it so that all four sides of the cabin will be true. Most cabins measure 16′ × 18′, 16′ × 20′, 20′ × 24′, or 20′ × 26′. Some builders add a lean-to for storage purposes or an additional bedroom.

Select 60 to 80 tall and straight trees, measuring 10 to 12 inches in diameter. Strip trees of branches and drag them to the cabin site. Choose four of the thickest logs to use as the foundation. Once the logs are notched at each end, actual raising can take place. To close the spaces between the logs, cut strips of wood to fit into the large openings. Then fill cracks with mud or clay mixed with the grass or straw.

Doors and Windows

Frames for the door, windows, and the fireplace

In northwest Iowa, where there were almost no trees, pioneers used the earth itself, or the sod, to make homes. They plowed it up in careful strips, cutting the strips into pieces about twelve inches long. Then they placed the strips of sod to form the outline of a house. Once the outline was in place, the settlers laid strip upon strip to build up the walls.

may be hewn from straight logs. Iowans can benefit from the increased supply of glass and hardware. Both items can be purchased from hardware and lumber dealers in Iowa's cities. Itinerant merchants carry glass and hardware. Some will take orders for their next trip to your area.

Roof

The roof may be made of hewn logs with straw used as a temporary cover. Shingles may be stripped from logs to form a permanent roof.

Fireplace

The fireplace is an important part of the cabin. It provides heat for cooking purposes and warmth plus light at night. Stones covered with clay mud make the safest fireplaces. Some make a temporary fireplace out of logs covered with clay on the inside. However, the latter type is a fire hazard.

Puncheon Flooring

Dirt floors may be covered by preparing logs for a smooth surface. Split logs and hew the flat side with your broad axe or adze. Place the logs side by side with the rounded side on the soil. The logs soon settle into the soil and you have a smooth walking surface. The floor is also warmer. [*1870 Iowa State Almanac*]

A pioneer family outside their sod house in Osceola County, 1872.

HOW TO BUILD A SOD HOUSE

In much of Iowa timber is scarce. The prairie sod makes a good substitute for building homes. The first step in building a soddie is to mow an acre or so of grass. Then hitch the horses or oxen to a grasshopper plow. This type of plow turns over a strip of sod from 3 to 6 inches thick and a foot wide. Once it is turned over, use a sharp spade to chop the strip into the right lengths.

The first layer of sod is very important. It forms the foundation. Place the strips, grassy side down, to make the outline of the house. Then level the first layer and place the second layer over it. Make a double row of sod strips so that the walls are from 2 feet to 30 inches thick. A fireplace of sod strips may be built on one wall. A few pieces of lumber will serve as the door and window

Families lived in soddies for years, discovering that the houses were cool in the summer and warm in the winter. People in sod houses did have to watch out for some things, however, especially insects and snakes. One man remembered that when it rained, he had to hold an umbrella over the stove so his mother could cook without any uninvited guests falling into the food.

Most settlers could not afford to bring many things with them on the long journey to Iowa. Sarah Kenyon, who came with her husband, John, wrote back to her relatives in the East:

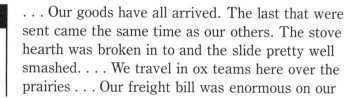

> . . . Our goods have all arrived. The last that were sent came the same time as our others. The stove hearth was broken in to and the slide pretty well smashed. . . . We travel in ox teams here over the prairies . . . Our freight bill was enormous on our

frames. The resourceful builder will find enough lumber in nearby towns or railroad supply centers.

The difficult feature is the roof. Pieces of lumber or timber are placed over the top of the walls. It must have the right slope. It is too steep, the strips will slide off. If it is not steep enough, the water will not run off in a heavy rain. On the roof, the sod is placed grassy side up. In the spring, the sod roof turns green and in the summer prairie flowers bloom. It is wise to check root growth on the roof. Growing roots cause water to trickle down into the house.

The owner of the sod house will find it warm in the winter and cool in the summer. Prairie winds will not topple a sod house. And its best feature is its cost. Reports to the editors show $15.00 to be top cost. [*1870 Iowa State Almanac*]

goods but I don't see what we could have spared very well. We get along with what we brought. All that I brought was a half dozen cups and saucers.
—Sarah B. Kenyon
Plum Creek August 29, 1856

When the Kenyons first arrived in Iowa there were no stores where they could buy supplies so families had to make or grow almost everything they needed. In many ways, a pioneer farm was like a group of tiny factories. Pioneers grew most of their own food and made most of their own clothing. They even made their own sweetener by growing sorghum for molasses. When candles and soap had to be made by hand, people were careful not to waste anything.

Men and women usually had different jobs. Women worked in the house and garden while men planted the

All that I brought was a half dozen cups and saucers.
—Sarah Kenyon (pioneer, Delaware County, 1856)

63

crops and cared for the animals. Sons were raised to do the same work as their fathers, and daughters were raised to do the same as their mothers. Almost all work was thought of as either men's work or women's work.

WOMEN'S WORK: TENDING THE HOUSE AND GARDEN

Food

Pioneer women spent most time growing, preserving, and preparing food. Each woman planted a large garden, sometimes one-half acre in size, with carrots, radishes, lettuce, pumpkins, and beans. Potatoes were so important as food that people often planted a small field of them. Children helped weed the garden and pick the vegetables.

Many of the vegetables were dried and stored for winter. If they were not dried properly, they might rot in the root cellar. This was a large hole dug in the ground and covered with wooden boards. Here the vegetables were sandwiched between layers of straw or sawdust to feed the family until the next spring. As well as growing and preserving food, pioneer mothers also baked bread and churned butter.

Many pioneer families complained that their diets were always the same. That was especially true in the winter when people had to go for months without fresh fruits or vegetables. Even during the summer, however, people still ate the same foods day after day. Two of these foods were corn and pork. Corn could be fixed many different ways, including johnnycakes (like pancakes), hominy, corn bread, and cornmeal mush. Sometimes mush was served for breakfast, then reheated and served at both the noon and evening meals. Pork was processed

64

by cooking and salting it and then packing it into crocks sealed with melted lard. If they had more time, pioneers also smoked the pork, especially the hams, to improve the flavor. During the winter months, some families ate salt pork at every meal. Elizabeth Koren, who lived in northeast Iowa in the 1850s, wrote in her diary that she often had to eat salt pork three times a day. She finally wrote that if she was served salt pork one more time, she thought that she would scream!

When spring arrived on the Iowa prairie, the pioneers looked forward to seeing something green come out of the earth. Eager to taste anything fresh, they ate dandelion greens, lamb's quarters, and colt's foot. In the spring, mothers gave their children a big dose of sulfur and molasses to thin down their blood. The mothers believed that during the winter, their children's blood had thickened.

> Finished ironing, baked bread and a cream pudding, cooked a chicken pot pie, corn and potatoes for dinner, mopped, etc. . . . Have dressed 12 pigeons and 18 chickens today.
> —Mary St. John (Iowa farm woman, 1858)

Clothing

Mothers on the Iowa frontier spent long hours making cloth and sewing. Making cloth was a slow process. First, someone had to shear the sheep and pick and card the wool. The next step was to spin the yarn on the spinning wheel. After that, women set up their looms and wove the yarn into cloth. We do not know how long it took Iowa women to make cloth and sew a suit of clothes, but a woman in Connecticut recorded that when her son needed a suit of clothes, she wove the cloth and made the suit in one week.

As well as weaving and sewing, women spent a great deal of time mending clothes. Mending was important when each member of the family had only a few items of clothing. One pioneer from a large family wrote that his mother found it hard to keep up with mending.

He remembered so many holes in their clothes that when company arrived, his mother made him and his younger brother run into the woods and hide.

Of all their work, pioneer mothers especially dreaded washday. They often had to carry buckets of water from a nearby stream to their home. Some women solved this problem by carrying the clothes to the stream and washing them there. Washday often took two days. The first day, the women hauled the water to the cabin and the second day they actually washed the clothes. They used a scrubboard, which took a great deal of energy. As a result, everyone wore their clothes for a long time between washings. You waited, they said on the frontier, until "clothes were dirty enough to stand up by themselves in the corner."

Health

Because there were so few trained doctors on the frontier, pioneer women had to act as both doctors and nurses for their families. Women usually learned from their own mothers how to care for the sick. One of the treatments was to apply a poultice to bad cuts or infections. A poultice is a soft material, such as bread, that is heated and placed on a wound. Many women also grew herbs to make into teas and syrups for treating colds, sore throats, and other ailments. Some women, called midwives, also delivered babies.

In addition to their housework, women often did chores outside the cabin. They raised chickens, gathered the eggs, and helped milk the cows. After milking the cows, they separated the cream from the milk. Some women helped their husbands with farm work like picking corn. If a woman's husband died, she often had to take over all the farm work as well as doing the work inside the house.

State Historical Society

In 1861, twenty-three-year-old Emily Hawley came to Delaware County in eastern Iowa to keep house for her widowed uncle and his daughter. Her uncle kept an inn for stagecoach passengers, and Emily had to clean and cook. The next year Emily married a local farmer, James Gillespie, and started keeping a diary. For the next twenty years she wrote almost daily about her work, her husband, and her children.

After Emily and James were married, they lived with James's parents for several years. Emily helped with the farm work, doing both indoor and outdoor chores. "O dear, work, work, work all the time," she noted after two busy months. Emily and her mother-in-law often made extra money by serving food to travelers and giving them a place to sleep. Sometimes the Gillespies took in travelers two or three times a week. In October 1862, after eight travelers had stayed overnight and all the next day, Emily wrote in her diary: "It is about all Ma and me can do to cook and wait on them." She added, "The men paid Pa $9.00."

Two years later, the young Gillespies moved into their own farm home. Emily and James had two children. The first, Henry, was born in 1863. A neighbor woman delivered Henry and charged $2.00 for her work. A short while later Emily wrote in her diary: "Baby was born about half past ten A.M. then could we thank God for our boy." Two years later, Emily gave birth to a daughter, Sarah.

Emily's diary tells us that on Mondays she did all her regular housework before 9 A.M. Then she started scrubbing clothes on a scrubboard and usually finished the wash by 3 P.M. She also made clothes for her children and her husband. Often she writes about finishing a shirt for James or a dress for Sarah.

Every year Emily kept a garden and raised chickens and turkeys. Sometimes she helped her husband with outside farm work. She tells of selling items that she produced on the farm, including butter, eggs, cheese, and molasses. Over several years Emily raised seventy-five turkeys and sold them each for 75 cents. The money she made helped the family pay off their farm debt. At one time she made bonnets that she sold to other farm women, making a profit of $1.70 on each bonnet. Occasionally she did sewing for others.

Emily also tried to keep down her purchases. In 1864, she bought the tools with which to make shoes. In her diary she writes that she was happy that she could make shoes for her two small children and not have to buy them.

When we read her diary, we are not surprised to learn about the hard work of an Iowa farm woman, but it is surprising that Emily was able to sell so many different things. Her sale of eggs, cream, butter, and even bonnets brought many dollars into the home. We think of farm families making money from the sale of corn, pigs, and chickens but not of making money from keeping overnight visitors or from making bonnets.

MEN'S WORK: FARMING THE PRAIRIE

Crops

It sounded like many pistols going off.
— Iowa pioneer (on first breaking the prairie sod, 1830s)

On a pioneer farm, the outside work was determined by the season of the year. First, of course, the men plowed up the prairie sod. This was hard work because the thick prairie grasses had long roots. In 1837, John Deere invented a large steel plow that turned a deep,

68

wide furrow of black prairie dirt. Dirt slipped off the shiny steel, and this made the plowing go faster.

An Iowa pioneer farmer plowing the prairie for the first time.

Even with a better plow, turning the original prairie sod was difficult. It usually took several yokes of oxen to pull the plow through the field. When prairie sod was turned for the first time, it made loud popping sounds as the thousands of grass and plant roots snapped. One witness said that it sounded like pistols going off, while another compared it to the sound of ripping cloth.

Besides the main crop of corn, settlers planted a few acres of oats and barley to feed their animals. Most pioneer farms also included a few acres of wheat, which could be ground into flour for baking bread or sold to bring in a little money. There was usually a small field of potatoes to feed the family. Out of eighty acres, a pioneer farmer might have forty acres planted in crops. He would also cut and stack hay as winter feed for his livestock.

69

Of all the work that farmers had to do, picking corn was the hardest. In the fall, the entire family helped pick, usually dropping the ripe ears into a large sack hung over one shoulder. Later on, the ears of corn would be thrown into a large wagon pulled by horses trained to walk through the fields at the same pace as the pickers. If an early snow made it impossible to finish the harvest, the corn was left standing, to be picked in the spring.

Livestock

Because corn was too bulky to haul to distant markets, farmers fed the grain to hogs and then sold the hogs. Sometimes farmers drove the hogs to market for sale. Otherwise they butchered them and carted the frozen meat to market on a sled.

Farm families also butchered meat for their own use. This had to be done when it was so cold that the meat would not spoil. Neighbors often got together to help, and among them, pioneers made use of every part of the pig, even the knuckles, bristles, and skin.

LEISURE ACTIVITIES

Many people believe that the pioneers were lonely and isolated. In fact, pioneer life in some parts of our country was more difficult than in others. For example, settlers in South Dakota and Nebraska could be cut off from other people. But once settlement started in Iowa, the whole state filled up rapidly. This meant that farms were close together and families often visited back and forth. Pioneers might have missed family and friends back East, but in Iowa they were not alone on the prairie. People helped one another with farm work and in times of trouble. When someone died, neighbors came in to prepare the body for the funeral and to help out with the farm chores.

Both pioneer men and women met other people fairly often. Men went to town more than women, usually to buy goods from the local store and to take care of business matters. Women visited their neighbors, sometimes packing up their mending and their youngest children and staying for the entire day. Women exchanged work with other women, which gave them a chance to visit as well. One would sew while a friend cared for her child. Life for Iowa's early farm families may have been difficult, but it was not lonely.

By the 1870s, almost forty years after settlement started in Iowa, few farm families were still pioneers. Instead of producing their own food and making all their clothing, farmers sold their crops and animals. Families then had the money to go to town and buy supplies. Farm families learned they could make more money raising items to sell (commercial farming), rather than producing only what they needed themselves (subsistence farming).

By 1870, there were other changes in Iowa. The state now contained thousands of farms and hundreds of small towns. Farm families no longer had to be self-sufficient. They could travel to town for trade or social events. They could usually find a doctor in the nearby town and they could buy newspapers as well as food and clothing. As Iowa's pioneer period came to an end, town and country people began to mingle. The farmer needed the town merchants to provide supplies, and the merchants needed the farmer to buy their goods. Farm and town people still lived in different ways, but they had come to depend on each other.

FURTHER READING

Birch, Brian P. "Possessed of a Restless Spirit: A Young Girl's Memories of the Southern Iowa Frontier." *The Palimpsest* 66, no. 5 (September/October 1985). Iowa City: State Historical Society of Iowa.

Bonney, Margaret, ed. "Early Agriculture." *The Goldfinch* 2, no. 3 (February 1981). Iowa City: State Historical Society of Iowa.

Goranson, Rita. "Sod Dwellings in Iowa." *The Palimpsest* 65, no. 4 (July–August 1984). Iowa City: State Historical Society of Iowa.

Riley, Glenda. *Frontierswomen.* Ames: Iowa State University Press, 1981.

_____. "Prairie Partnerships." *The Palimpsest* 69, no. 2 (Summer 1988). Iowa City: State Historical Society of Iowa.

Rivers, Trails, and Train Tracks

TRANSPORTATION IN THE 1800s

How to get to Iowa was a problem for people planning to come here in the 1800s. The first settlers traveled on steamboats and stagecoaches and even walked from eastern states. Later, in the 1850s and 1860s, they were able to travel on railroads. Once people had settled the land and started farming, they needed ways to ship their crops to market. Business people also needed ways to ship goods from the East to stores in Iowa. During the nineteenth century, Iowans tried different types of transportation and came to rely most heavily on railroads.

STEAMBOATS

In 1807, Robert Fulton built the first steamboat, named the *Clermont,* in New York state. Soon steamboats appeared on rivers in the Midwest. Fulton's invention was important because it allowed people to travel faster. It had always been simple to float downriver with the current. The difficult job was traveling upriver *against* the current, and the steamboat solved that problem.

The first steamboat appeared on the upper Mississippi River (north of St. Louis) in 1823. Soon boats were going upriver carrying food and guns from St. Louis to forts in Iowa and Minnesota. Boats going downriver along Iowa's eastern border carried furs and lead ore.

Before long, steamboats started to carry another cargo—people. Settlers coming into Iowa by steamboat, rather than by covered wagon, could bring along more furniture and other belongings. People traveling to Iowa from New York or Pennsylvania often took the Ohio River to St. Louis. There, they boarded a steamboat going up the Mississippi to Iowa. Immigrants from Europe would come to New Orleans to take steamboats headed upriver. It took about three weeks to travel from New Orleans to Burlington, Iowa.

The main reason immigrants traveled by steamboats was the low cost. People could have individual cabins called staterooms if they paid more, and cabin passengers ate their meals in the dining room. But immigrants usually chose to travel deck passage, which cost one-fourth as much as cabin passage.

Deck passage had its drawbacks. Immigrants had to stay on the lowest deck. Sometimes there were bunks, but often they just slept on the deck itself. The deck was crowded, not only with people but with machinery, cargo, and sometimes animals. Deck passengers had to carry their own food. Many boats had only one or two stoves on which the immigrants could cook, so often they simply ate their food cold. Sometimes even water was not available.

Steamboat travel could be dangerous. If the boat's boiler (which made the steam) got too hot and exploded, nearby passengers were scalded with hot water. Steamboats sometimes caught fire. The pilot then tried to run

Going along at a snail gallop.
—William Buxton, (steamboat traveler, 1853)

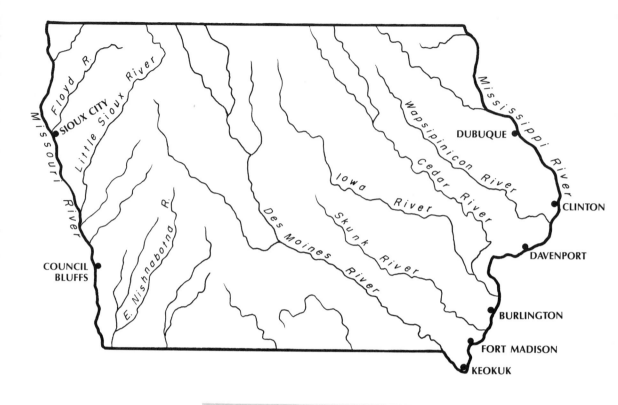

Iowa is sometimes called the "land between two rivers" because its eastern and western borders are formed by the Mississippi and the Missouri, two of the most important rivers in America. In the state's early history, steamboats carried people and goods up and down these water highways. The first settlers came by way of the river towns, which are still among the largest cities in the state. Barges full of grain, meat, and flour from Iowa farms floated down to the city of New Orleans to be loaded onto ships headed for eastern American cities and Europe.

Once railroads crossed the Mississippi River, river traffic decreased. Trains linking Iowa to Chicago and the East could transport Iowa farm products more quickly than steamboats. Unlike river traffic, they could run throughout the year. When the railroads came, Iowa's days as a frontier state were over.

74

the boat ashore so passengers could jump over the side. Many boats sank when they hit snags or floating logs.

Sometimes steamboat passengers caught cholera, a deadly disease. Cholera is an illness that causes dehydration (loss of water from the body). People became ill very quickly. It was possible to feel fine in the morning and to be extremely sick by that night. Many cholera victims died in three or four days. Ships coming from foreign countries brought cholera into the United States. When infected people got on steamboats, other passengers and people along the way would be exposed to the disease. There were major outbreaks of cholera in 1832 and 1848.

The Diamond Jo Line was one of the main steamboat companies operating on the upper Mississippi River.

Steamboat captains did not want people to know that their boats carried cholera victims because it would mean a loss of business. The crew might even desert the boat if they knew. So when a victim died, the captain might make a quick stop along shore to bury the body. Others just dumped the body in the river. Ships with cholera were called "pest boats" and people were afraid to travel on them.

There was steamboat traffic on the Missouri River as well as on the Mississippi. In 1866, the steamboat *Bertrand* was carrying supplies for a general store in Montana when it hit a snag and sank. The river covered it with a layer of mud, which preserved the boat's cargo for a century. In 1965, the *Bertrand* was dug up from the river. Its contents—the tools, clothing, medicine bottles, and cans of food that would have been sold to western pioneers—are now on display in a museum at De Soto Bend in western Iowa.

Steamboats provided the main means of transportation for Iowans until the 1870s. By then, railroads had been built across the state and most people preferred to travel by train. People also chose to travel from the East by railroad. After 1870, passengers still traveled on steamboats, but often for fun rather than for business.

Crowd gathered to watch a Mississippi River steamboat, around 1910. People in Dubuque and Davenport and other river cities often spent the Fourth of July riding a steamboat up and down the river.

State Historical Society

STAGECOACHES

While steamboats chugged up and down the rivers, stagecoaches carried people and mail into the rest of Iowa. From 1833 to around 1870, the main stage lines ran east and west across the state. They provided service between cities, such as Dubuque and Cedar Falls, Cedar Rapids and Clinton, and Davenport and Council Bluffs.

The Western Stage Company was the largest stagecoach line in the state. It owned many large, comfortable vehicles known as Concord Stages. The oval-shaped Concord Stage was set on heavy strips of leather that acted as springs and made the ride less bumpy. Concord coaches had three seats that each held three people. The driver might decide to carry even more passengers, so sometimes people rode on top of the stage, sitting on the mailbags.

Stagecoaches and covered wagons were two main ways to travel before railroads were built across Iowa.

The Western Stage Company operated throughout Iowa, Wisconsin, Missouri, and eastern Nebraska. Because of its size, the company hired about 1,500 people and owned 3,000 horses and 600 coaches. About every fifteen miles, the company set up a stage stop where passengers could eat and sleep and where the driver could change horses.

Along with the Western Stage Company, Iowa had several smaller stage lines. These companies could not afford the Concord stages and instead used open wagons. Often they put a cloth cover over the top, which made the stages look like the covered wagons that carried people on the Oregon trail.

Stagecoach travel was uncomfortable. During the mid-1800s when stages traveled through Iowa, there were few roads. Usually the stage followed bumpy trails across the countryside. Sometimes the horses were frightened by noises or wild animals and ran away with the stage. Passengers told about stages tipping over, so that everyone had to get out and help put them right side up. Even with pleasant weather and good roads, the trip was long and boring at 3½ miles per hour.

Passengers often traveled for several days, which meant they had to stay in stagecoach stops. They complained that the stations were dirty and served bad food. Often there were not enough beds for everyone so three people had to sleep together. This meant that people were sleeping with total strangers.

One stagecoach company published a list of tips for travelers.

Don't swear or fall over neighbors when sleeping.
Never shoot on the road as the noise might frighten the horses.
Don't point out where murders have been

78

committed, especially if there are women passengers.

Stagecoaches operated in Iowa only until railroads were built across the state. Railroad travel was faster and more pleasant than stage travel. In 1870, Western Stage went out of business—a sure sign that over thirty years of stagecoach travel had come to an end in Iowa.

Journal of William Buxton: An Account of His Travels from Nottingham, England, to Carlisle, Iowa, November 7 to December 25, 1853

[William Buxton, a native of Derbyshire, England, migrated to the United States in 1851 at the age of twenty-one. He settled in Carlisle, Iowa, where he bought a quarter section of land (160 acres). Two years later, his uncle in England died, leaving him $2,000 in cash. He returned to England to claim his inheritance. On his trip back to the United States, he kept a daily account of his travel experiences. This is part of his journal.]

Monday, November 7.	Left Nottingham early, on my return voyage to the land of the West. . . . I received the last well wishes of the many friends I have learned to value. . . .
Tuesday, November 8.	Tuesday arrived in Liverpool and took passage in the screw steamship "City of Glasgow" for Philadelphia. . . .
Friday, November 11.	Irish coast in view, head wind and clear sky pretty rough sea nearly all sick, myself among [the] lot dreadfully sick and good for nothing vowed never to cross again except on my return. Course N.W. run 192 [miles].

Saturday, November 12.	Feeling rather curious but after eating a good dinner was as fresh and content as ever. Course West run 188 [miles]. Wednesday midnight we had a most hairbreadth escape of being run down by a large [vessel] in full sail which came so close as to carry away part of our rigging; a few feet nearer we should have met with certain destruction. . . .
Tuesday, November 15.	Fine, getting quite jolly and friendly now on board spending the day in reading and games [and] the evenings in concerts. course N.W. Run 199 [miles].
Thursday, November 17.	All quiet again today very glad to see it so and now begin to relish the meals which are served up as follows. breakfast at 8 & 9 dinner 1 & 3 supper 6 & 7 o'clock provided on a very liberal scale C. West run 146 mls.
Friday, November 18.	Past a very rough night, the sea now running what is term'd mountains high, the finest I have ever seen, hope it may not last long, too cold to be on deck. . . . Run 190 mls. . . . At dinner . . . some unfortunate dish would come sliding majestically on to the floor, and requiring some effort to keep one's seat at the table. . . .
Sunday, November 20.	Dry and cold moderate & favorable wind as we are passed at 8 p.m. by a mail steamer which left N. York last Wednesday signals were given & returned rockets were first thrown up from our ship and answered by the same number from the other. . . .Run 200 mls.
Monday, November 21.	Fine & pleasant & fair wind 12 p.m. run 209 mls. This evening we had our celebrated concert commencing at 7½

80

o'clock. . . . After the concert the company adjourned to the quarter deck to witness the fireworks which were very imposing. Then came the dance, concluding with supper in saloon. . . .

Wednesday, November 23. 12 p.m. Last night we had the first theatrical performance on board the comic farce of Box & Box & Mrs. Bouncer the lodging housekeeper. . . .

Friday, November 25. Last night the wind got up blowing strong, the sea changing in a few hours from a perfect calm to the opposite extreme but settled down considerably this morning. passed a beautiful clipper built ship hoisted American colors. Looking out for pilot boat, Run 233 mls. . . . the land appeared ahead Cape May on our right. The shore all along is low and sandy. Philadelphia lies about 100 miles up the Delaware a fine broad stream with a fine country on both sides. We anchored in the river at night and came along side the pier about 1 o'clock Saturday making a passage of seventeen days 3275 miles.

Saturday, November 26. . . . Took a [tour] through the City, which is one of the finest in The States. . . . I think the ladies of Philadelphia surpass anything I ever saw in any other city for beauty and dress.

Tuesday, November 29. Took ticket for Cincinnati via Baltimore and Ohio rail to Wheeling then a boat on the river. Left Phil. at 2 p.m. arriving at Wheeling 2½ p.m. Wednesday 490 miles. The railroad runs direct over the Alegany mountains almost impassable, winding round the hills and overlooking some precipices truly fearful and certain

81

	death in case of any mishap one journey is quite sufficient to satisfy any traveller especially when he knows that the works are anything but substantial.
Wednesday, November 30.	Left Wheeling at 4 p.m. by the [steamboat] "Latrobe," should be in Cincinnati early on Friday but am afraid I shall be disappointed. . . .
Thursday, December 1.	Going along at a snail gallop. . . .
Friday, December 2.	Moving slowly down the river expecting every minute to come to a stand, several other boats being fast and stopping the navigation. In the evening most of the passengers were prevailed upon to go ashore in order to lighten a little and a good part of the freight put ashore but notwithstanding every endeavor the boat stuck fast alongside four others near Buffenden Island. . . .
Saturday, December 2.	Still fast and with every prospect of a famine on board. Hearing of a boat being below, for Cincinnati we all left the "Latrobe" sending our baggage and the ladies down in canoes. The gents walked down to the boat. The "Crystal Palace" a splendid boat, good fare, which they took care to get paid for many of the passengers having to pay a second full fare however I was glad to get off on any terms.
Sunday, December 4.	Arrived late in evening at Cincinnati.
Monday, December 12.	. . . went to see the pork slaughter yards which is carried on here on a large scale, a thousand hogs being a day's work for one set of hands to kill & pack, but rather roughly done.

82

Tuesday, December 13.	Got on the "Ben Franklin" for Louisville and St. Louis, which left at 12 p.m. reaching Louisville in twelve hours 15 mls.
Wednesday, December 14.	Took the [horse-drawn] bus down to Portland since round the falls the water being too low to allow the boats to pass over, and got aboard the "Fashion" for St. Louis 700 mls from Cincinnati entered the Mississippi Friday noon. Took on a lot of Californians at Cairo bound home, some with a good "pile" others with disappointed hopes only.
Sunday, December 18.	Arrived early this morning at St. Louis winter having set in hard pretty near closed navigation on the upper river.
Monday, December 19.	. . . started off at 6 p.m. for Keokuk 215 mls on the "Dubuque," probably the last boat to ascend the Mississippi this season – it being both difficult & dangerous on account of the ice which is fast choking up the river and very thick in some places. The upper Mississippi is far more interesting than the lower (so far as I have been) beautifully studded with islands and fine high bluffs. The water above the Missouri is perfectly clear and transparent.
Wednesday, December 21.	Morning arrived safe at Keokuk the end of my river travelling and very glad of it. In time of high water it is very pleasant but miserable at low stages. Most of the captains & inferior officers are generally nothing but a lot of sharpers!
Thursday, December 22.	Had to lie over until Thursday morning for the stage which left at 4 a.m. for Fort D'Moines 180 mls.

Saturday, December 24.	The roads being good we got on pretty fast, travelling it in three days, first night at Fairfield, 2nd, Oskaloosa where we just came in right for a bear meat supper and ball the first was excellent, the latter very commonplace. Arrived at the Fort about seven Saturday evening, pretty well tired of the stage.
Sunday, December 25.	Xmas day walked over to Carlisle 12 mls, which is to be my future home.

[William Buxton later married Betsy Bramhall, and they farmed outside Carlisle for forty years. For seventeen of those years, the Buxtons and their five children (four girls and one boy) lived in a log cabin, before they built a frame house. Mr. Buxton died in Indianola in 1919 at the age of eighty-nine. He owned 1,400 acres of farmland at the time of his death.]

RAILROADS

In the 1850s, Iowans began to think about railroads. The first railroad in America had been built in 1831 in Baltimore so merchants could ship their goods to western Maryland. At first, people laughed at the idea that trains (which traveled fifteen miles an hour) would replace horses and buggies. Before long, however, they stopped joking about the "iron horse," and instead worked to bring railroads to their towns.

During the 1850s, four railroads were built from Chicago to the Mississippi River (the western border of Illinois). Iowans could see that if railroads were built from the Mississippi (Iowa's eastern border) across Iowa they would link up with the Illinois railroads. Then Iowans could ship their farm goods to Chicago and on to eastern states by rail. From the east coast, Iowa goods could be shipped to foreign countries. Everyone in the state would benefit from building railroads.

People in the river cities began to hold public meetings to discuss forming railroad companies. Citizens in Dubuque, Clinton, Davenport, and Burlington all planned railroads that would extend across the state and could connect with a railroad in western Illinois. But it took time and a great deal of money to build a railroad. Dubuque citizens held their first railroad meeting in 1853. They started building in 1855. Two years later they had graded only thirty-eight miles of roadbed. By 1870, the Dubuque and Pacific Railroad finished its construction across the state. In all, it took seventeen years to construct a railroad a distance of four hundred miles.

As people began to travel by railroad, hotels such as the Roberts House (shown here in 1890) were built.

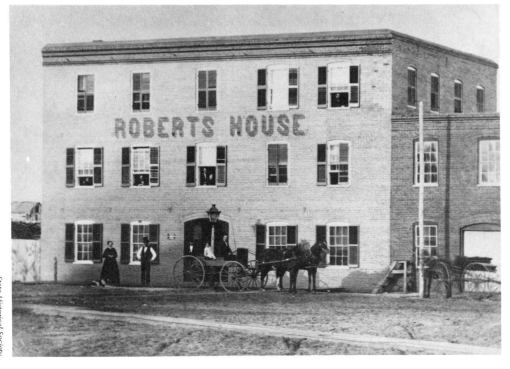

The biggest problem faced by Iowa's railroad builders was raising money. The Dubuque and Pacific planners asked all Dubuque citizens and people living nearby to contribute money or land to the railroad. They also received aid from the United States government.

In 1856, the government gave Iowa a land grant of four million acres to help raise money for railroad construction. This land was then divided between four railroads in the state: the Burlington, the Chicago and North Western, the Rock Island, and the Illinois Central (which took over the Dubuque and Pacific). Each of these railroads could sell its land whenever it wished. The Dubuque and Pacific Railroad, short on money from the beginning, quickly sold much of its land for $8.50 an acre. The Burlington was able to keep its land longer and eventually received about $12 an acre.

As railroads built westward, they linked up towns along the way. People often held big celebrations to welcome the railroad. When the Dubuque and Pacific reached Waterloo in 1861, the local newspaper reported:

 It was a signal for a general celebration, as it put an end to long overland trips to Dubuque to market goods and secure supplies. . . . The railroad brought [people] luxuries, conveniences they had not known before, not even in their former homes in the East.

When the Civil War started in 1861, railroad building in Iowa stopped. Because so many men went into the army, the railroad crews were short of workers. Also, the government needed rails and other equipment for war purposes. But shortly after the war ended, construction crews again started laying tracks across the state.

The Illinois Central started in Chicago and ended at the Mississippi River across from the city of Dubuque. In 1867 it bought out the Dubuque line and formed one major railroad. Once this merger (combining two businesses) was complete, the Illinois Central had the funds to finish the route across Iowa, ending in Sioux City. In fact, the Illinois Central kept right on going until it reached Fremont, Nebraska. There it linked up with the Union Pacific, a larger railroad that went across Nebraska and into the far west. Reaching the Union Pacific was important because then people in northern Iowa could travel all the way to California.

GRENVILLE DODGE

Grenville Dodge was a famous railroad builder. In his lifetime, he helped build over sixty thousand miles of track, including the Union Pacific, which linked the east coast with the West.

Dodge was born in Massachusetts in 1831. As a boy, he delivered meat and clerked in a store. Later, he studied to become an engineer. Engineers then surveyed land and planned roads and bridges. In 1852, Dodge took a job with the Mississippi and Missouri Railroad (later the Rock Island). At that time, railroad building had not started in Iowa. Dodge surveyed a route from Davenport to Iowa City and then across the state to Council Bluffs. He finished surveying in 1853 and decided to live in Council Bluffs. There he opened a store and a bank and traded with Indian tribes to the west in Nebraska. He also did some railroad surveying west of the Missouri River.

When the Civil War began, Dodge joined the Union Army. His skill at building bridges and railroad tracks helped to move Northern troops more rapidly to the front lines where they were desperately needed. In Tennessee, Dodge and his men won the praise of General Ulysses

Grant, commander of the northern army, by rebuilding 182 bridges and repairing 102 miles of railroad track in just forty days. Even President Abraham Lincoln asked his advice on railroad construction. By the end of the war, Dodge had been promoted to major general.

After the war, General Dodge became chief engineer of the Union Pacific Railroad. The Union Pacific was building a line from Council Bluffs across the West to meet the Central Pacific Railroad, which had started eastward from Sacramento, California. The two railroads finally met at Promontory Point, Utah, and a great celebration was held. Americans could finally travel from one coast to the other by train.

When Dodge had finished working on the Union Pacific, he served one term in the U.S. Congress. Then he supervised the building of new rail lines in Texas and the Southwest. After 1900, he even helped organize a railroad company in Cuba.

As a result of his railroad work and business interests, Dodge became a very rich man. He built a mansion in Council Bluffs that was one of the finest homes in Iowa. Dodge died there in 1916. Today, the Grenville Dodge home is open as a museum.

The Illinois Central also began to build new towns. When the Civil War ended in 1865, the eastern half of Iowa was covered with towns, but the western half had only a few communities. The Illinois Central, like Iowa's other main railroads, built towns along the way. It was important to have people living along the route because the railroad needed people to travel on their line and to ship agricultural products eastward.

Between Iowa Falls and Sioux City, the Illinois Central laid out over twenty towns. Most of them were twelve to eighteen miles apart, for example, Alta to

Cherokee – 15 miles, Cherokee to Marcus – 14 miles, Marcus to Remsen – 12 miles, and Remsen to LeMars – 12 miles.

In planning towns, the railroads first decided just where they would be. Surveyors then made a plat (map) marking off the individual lots. Next, railroad officials set a date for an auction and advertised the date widely. People came from near and far to attend the auctions. Anyone who wanted to start a business in the new town bought lots both for their business and for their home. As soon as the auction ended, people began moving into the new community. Some towns were created overnight.

Hard as they tried, the Illinois Central was not the first railroad to finish building across Iowa. Three years before it reached Sioux City in 1870, the Chicago and North Western Railroad reached Council Bluffs. By 1870, all four major railroads had reached the state's western border.

After 1870, Iowans continued to build railroads, but usually lines that ran north-south rather than east-west, and short lines (called spur lines) that connected nearby towns to a main railroad. Shorter railroads, called commuter lines or interurbans, were built to provide service from small to large towns. Every day the interurban ran from Des Moines to Fort Dodge with several stops along the way. Many people rode this train, traveling to Fort Dodge or Des Moines to shop, to seek medical care, or for business.

The luxury, convenience and solid comfort afforded by the [dining] cars will be fully appreciated . . . Strictly First-class Meals only 75 Cents.
— C.B.&Q. advertisement (1870s)

A crowd waits to meet the train at the Central City railroad depot, around 1901.

Advertisement for the Chicago, Burlington & Quincy line from an Iowa railroad travel guide.

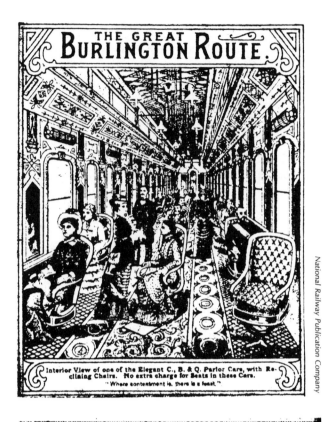

Interior View of one of the Elegant C., B. & Q. Parlor Cars, with Reclining Chairs. No extra charge for Seats in these Cars.
"Where contentment is, there is a feast."

National Railway Publication Company

THE GREAT BURLINGTON ROUTE

CHICAGO, BURLINGTON & QUINCY R. R.

PARLOR CARS

Are Rolling Palaces indeed. They were recently built by the Chicago, Burlington & Quincy Railroad Company at their own shops, at Aurora, Illinois; are

RICHLY AND TASTILY FURNISHED

Throughout, and were constructed with a SPECIAL view to the comfort and convenience of our passengers. The frame-work is of black walnut, and the paneling of maple. They are handsomely carpeted, and are fitted with Horton's Patent RECLINING CHAIRS.

They contain many new and important features that are not found in the Chair Cars of any other line, among which are TWO large separate Dressing Rooms for Ladies, instead of one, also a large double Wash Bowl for Gentlemen, and a commodious BAGGAGE and PARCEL ROOM, with a Porter in charge. Passengers upon entering the Car can deliver their hand baggage and Parcels to the Porter, who will *issue a check* for the same, thus entirely relieving the passenger from any further responsibility or trouble. Under this *new arrangement*, if passengers desire to leave the car for any purpose, they have no fear of their baggage being carried off, and on arrival at destination, in the event of their forgetting any portion of their baggage during the excitement (which is a very common occurrence), they still hold the Company's check for same, and have simply to send back the check and order the baggage forwarded by Express.

THE TOILET ROOMS

Are both elegant and complete. In each car are nine large chandeliers, thereby presenting a bright, cheerful and inviting appearance.

A Porter is in charge of each car, whose sole duty it is to attend to the wants of the passengers.

NO EXTRA CHARGE

Is made now for seats in these cars to those holding first-class tickets.

National Railway Publication Company

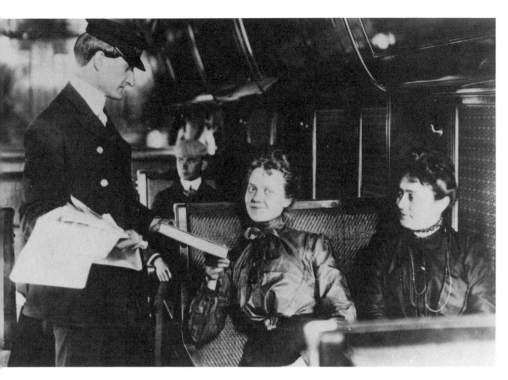

A conductor on the Chicago, Burlington & Quincy Railroad takes tickets from two passengers, around 1900.

The completion of Iowa's four main railroads was important for all Iowans. For the first time, people could travel comfortably in both winter and summer. Iowa's farmers had year-round transportation on which they could send their crops and livestock to market. With steamboats, crops and animals often had to be reloaded several times before they reached market, and steamboats could not travel when the rivers froze.

The development of Iowa's railroads led to the development of other industries. Because all railroads burned coal in the nineteenth century, Iowans opened coal mines and coal mining became a major industry. Some railroads opened and operated their own mines, called captive mines.

The development of railroads also led to the beginning of farm-related industries. Those are industries that use farm products or produce goods for sale to farmers. After railroads had been built across the state, meatpacking houses opened in cities like Sioux City, Des Moines, Waterloo, and Ottumwa. The railroads could haul the livestock and poultry to the plants and later carry the processed meat out to other parts of the country. Quaker Oats was another farm-related industry started in Iowa in the 1870s. Oats were taken to Cedar Rapids to be made into oatmeal. Today the Quaker Oats Company is one of the largest oats buyers in the world.

Railroads in Iowa led to the development of businesses such as the Sinclair Packing Company in Cedar Rapids.

Railroads also played an important role in transporting people. After the railroads received land grants in the 1850s, they were eager to sell their land. Some railroads put together cheap "immigrant trains" to bring people from New York and other eastern cities to Iowa. The railroads were hoping that the newcomers would buy railroad land and settle here. Many immigrants did just that and established farms along the railroad routes.

In the nineteenth century, Iowans learned that building different types of transportation was difficult and expensive. However, they developed steamboat and stagecoach lines and built railroads. Each took care of a particular need. Of all the types of transportation, however, railroads were by far the most important. With railroads, Iowans could travel faster and travel in all seasons. The railroads brought in new settlers, helped start new industries, and made life more pleasant for people. By 1900, cities and towns in Iowa were connected by railroads to the rest of the nation. State officials boasted by 1900 that no person anywhere in Iowa was more than eight miles from a railroad.

FURTHER READING

Bonney, Margaret, ed. "Railroads . . ." *The Goldfinch* 5, no. 2 (November 1983). Iowa City: State Historical Society of Iowa.

William Buxton Diary, 1853–1860. Ruth B. Sayre Collection. Iowa City: State Historical Society of Iowa.

Swaim, Ginalie, ed. "Rivers in Iowa." *The Goldfinch* 6, no. 4 (April 1985). Iowa City: State Historical Society of Iowa.

7 A Nation Divided

In the 1860s, Americans fought a civil war. It is difficult to understand completely why Americans in the North and South fought each other. But there are certain things we know about the views of the North and South and about Iowa's part in that conflict.

We know that slavery was one reason why people fought the war. Southern people owned about four million black (African-American) slaves in 1860. Southerners believed that there was nothing wrong with owning slaves and even that it was the proper way to live. Slavery was partly why eleven southern states left the Union (United States) to form their own government, the Confederate States of America. Northerners disagreed. They believed that slavery was wrong and that it should be ended.

We also know that many Iowans took part in the war. Seventy thousand Iowa men fought and many died or were badly wounded. Women also were involved in the war effort, making bandages, clothing, and food for the soldiers. Many took over farm work when their husbands went off to fight.

THE UNDERGROUND RAILROAD

Iowa became a state in 1846 and was known as a free state. That meant that slavery was not allowed here. Some Iowans were abolitionists (opposed to slavery and wanted it abolished). They believed that it was their duty to help runaway slaves get to Canada, where they would be free.

Many slaves headed for Canada, where their masters could not reclaim them. Some people in Iowa helped runaway slaves travel secretly across the state until they reached the Mississippi River. From there, they crossed into Illinois and then headed northward to Canada. This system of helping slaves to escape was called the "underground railroad," although it was neither underground nor a railroad.

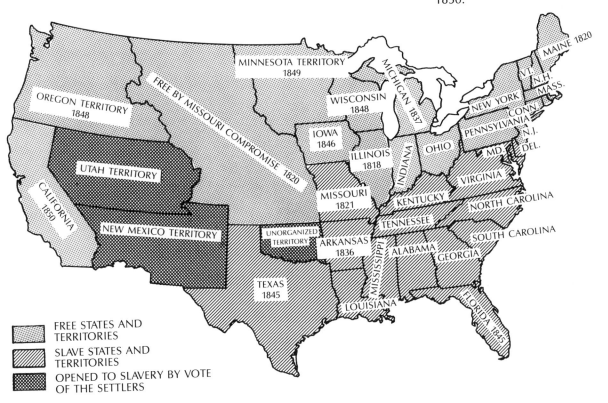

Free and slave areas in 1850.

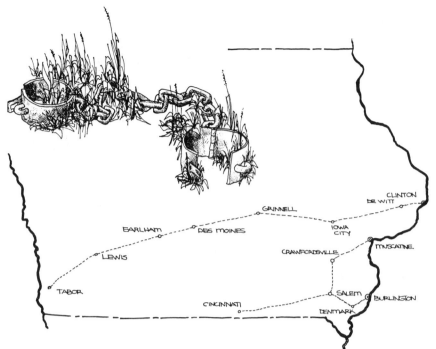

Underground railroad lines in Iowa.

Many who worked on the underground railroad were either Quakers or Congregationalists. These two religious groups hated slavery and believed that it was their duty to help slaves escape. The Reverend John Todd, a Congregational minister, was one of these people. He lived in Tabor, close to the Missouri River in southwest Iowa, and often moved slaves across Iowa. One time he dressed a black woman in Mrs. Todd's clothing to look like his wife, with a heavy veil across her face. They traveled by buggy across the state at night and on back roads. Many times escaping slaves would sleep in barns during the day and travel at night.

It is hard to know how many Iowans worked on the underground railroad, since people who did so were breaking the law. If caught, they might have to spend six months in jail or be forced to pay a fine of $1,000. Because of these penalties, Todd and others usually did not keep written records of how many slaves they helped. Most messages were quickly destroyed.

But even though most Iowans opposed slavery and some helped blacks escape from the South, Iowans did not want blacks to live here. That seems strange today, but in the nineteenth century Iowans believed that whites were better than blacks and that blacks and whites should live apart. For example, they believed that black children should go to segregated (separate) schools. Many people in other northern states held the same views. Today we call these racist views.

Before the Civil War, there were only a few blacks in Iowa. For example, in 1840 there were only 171, and most of them lived along the Mississippi or Missouri rivers. These black Iowans did not have many political rights, so they could not vote and their children could not attend the public schools.

The Iowa General Assembly had passed a law in 1847 making public schools "open and free alike to all white persons in the district between the ages of five and twenty-one years." In 1858, the General Assembly passed a school law stating that the district should provide separate schools for black children, unless the district's patrons all agreed to having a nonsegregated school. There were some segregated schools for blacks and whites as late as 1874.

A letter from Sarah Parker to her mother, describing a riot in Grinnell, shows the intense feelings that existed in 1860 over public schooling for African Americans (called "colored people" at the time).

> The question—"Shall colored pupils be received in our schools?" was put to vote at the school meeting, and the ayes carried it by a small majority.
> —Sarah Parker (Grinnell, 1860)

Grinnell, March 10, 1860

My Dear Mother,

Your letter, commenced on my birthday, is just received. . . . I have long been trying to write, but we have had a very interesting series of meetings, and when they closed, my eyes became sore so that I could not use them much, and am now just able to write. . . .

If my eyes were well and I had plenty of time and room, I would give you full particulars of, what think you!—THE FIRST MOB IN GRINNELL!

Do not be astonished; it *has* been and is gone, but its effects can never be effaced from our community. . . . Monday evening was a school meeting. To prepare you for what follows, I must relate a few facts. In the midst of our revival a Quaker brought for our safe keeping, four black men, whom the Tabor people helped to rescue from kidnappers. They were received, and offered work, as two of them wished to go back after their wives and children. They were anxious to learn and asked to go to school. Their employers consented to their going until the spring work came on. They went, but it offended many. The question—"Shall colored pupils be received in our schools?" was put to vote at the school meeting, and the ayes carried it by a small majority. One man arose in a frenzy of passion, exclaiming, "They shall never enter those doors unless over my dead body." Another says—"I go with you."—and still others said the same, telling the antislavery men they must come prepared to defend them if they send the negroes on. The proceedings of the meeting on the proslavery side were beyond belief. We . . . received torrents of abuse, ladies and all. . . . Mrs. Augusta Bixby, the Squire's wife received her portion with us, because she is a decided antislavery and lets it be known. Mr. Cooper was called a liar to his face—he only replied "Very well." . . . It was feared the meeting would not end without fighting—but it did.

Tuesday morning, between eight and nine, the mob came on to the school house, led by two of the most desperate men in town. The two negroes saw the proceedings and it roused their savage wrath. They armed themselves and came on, saying that if they must suffer so to gain their freedom, and have all these indignities heaped upon them after they had gained it, they might as well die at once. As the Blacks approached, the leaders of the mob went to

98

the schoolhouse steps with clubs, and it is supposed, concealed weapons. By much persuasion, the negroes were prevented from attempting to meet them, but it was their preference to fight their way through. They would probably have killed their leaders. Then the mob called on the officers to disarm them, but they would not, for their lives had been threatened and they would not deprive them of the means of defense. Riot ran wild in our streets until noon, then a short calm ensued. Meetings for counsel were held on both sides – secret meetings by the mob, in which Mr. Parker and the negroes were the objects on which to vent their wrath.

Wednesday forenoon was as exciting as the day before. Desperate deeds were meditated – men maddened with hate and rage ran through the streets with insulting words ever on their lips. When I bade my husband good morning, I did not know but he would be the first victim of the fury. For he told the mob the day before that if they attempted to touch one of the pupils under his care, he should defend him. But we all live – though knives were whetted for hand to hand encounters, guns loaded and pistols made ready.

God restrains wrath when his purpose is accomplished. The town is not settled yet. We know not what to do. It will probably divide the church for several of the members were in the mob. The school, closed on account of the trouble, is to commence in three weeks.

– Sarah Parker

THE CIVIL WAR

When the war started in April 1861, President Abraham Lincoln asked for 75,000 men to join the army. Lincoln thought the war would last only a few months and told the men that they would be home by Christmas. Each state had a quota (share) of men. Iowa's quota was about 800 and almost immediately it was filled with volunteers.

Ten men from Olin who served as soldiers in the Civil War.

The Second Iowa Infantry Regiment was one of the Iowa groups that fought in the war. This regiment was formed in April 1861 and was first sent to Missouri. There, even before the men reached the battlefront, many contracted measles and mumps and some died of these diseases. Men also got sick because of bad food.

From Missouri, the Second Iowa Regiment was sent on to Tennessee to fight under General U. S. Grant. They were at the capture of Fort Donelson, fought at Shiloh, and helped General Grant take Vicksburg, Mississippi. Vicksburg was an important victory because then the Union Army controlled the Mississippi River.

100

After Vicksburg, soldiers of the Second Iowa Regiment traveled on to Georgia where they fought for five days to take the city of Atlanta. The men then marched with General William Sherman to Savannah, Georgia, which was on the Atlantic Ocean. This was called "the March to the Sea." In this way, the Union army cut the South completely in half. Along the way, Union troops destroyed southern property to weaken the South.

From Savannah, the men of the Second Iowa Regiment were ordered to Washington, D.C., where they heard that the war was over. The weary men, many of them sick, headed home where they were mustered (released) out of the army.

Many Iowa soldiers, like soldiers elsewhere, were badly injured. It took months to get well. If a man was injured, he needed a family to care for him because the federal government did not have programs to help. But even though they suffered the rest of their lives from war injuries, the men were still proud that they had fought to keep the Union together.

Iowa soldiers fought in the Battle of Corinth in Tennessee in 1862.

While most men served as privates and corporals in the Union army, some Iowans served as officers. Grenville Dodge, who had built railroads in Iowa before the war, became a general. Dodge was involved with intelligence work (spying) for the Union Army. It was Dodge's job to get northern agents into the South. Then these people, both men and women, reported back on the movements of southern troops. This information often told Dodge where the Confederates were planning an attack.

Many soldiers kept diaries of their life in the army. Just after he had fought in the Battle of Pea Ridge, Arkansas, in 1862, Vinson Holmes wrote:

> I went up to see the Battle field and saw a great many dead bodies yet unburied. They were collected together and the soldiers were burying [them]. They looked horrible and they were terrible mangled and

CYRUS CARPENTER

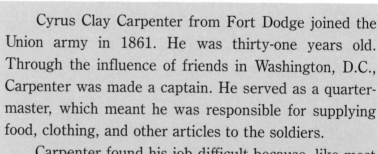

Cyrus Clay Carpenter from Fort Dodge joined the Union army in 1861. He was thirty-one years old. Through the influence of friends in Washington, D.C., Carpenter was made a captain. He served as a quartermaster, which meant he was responsible for supplying food, clothing, and other articles to the soldiers.

Carpenter found his job difficult because, like most of the other soldiers, he had never been in the army and had no special training. He had to feed 40,000 men and he found it hard to get enough food and to move the food supplies to keep up with the soldiers. In his diary, Carpenter tells how he once had to burn a large amount of food to keep it out of the hands of Confederate soldiers.

Seven years after the war, Carpenter was elected governor of Iowa.

covered with blood and gore . . . dead horses were strewn all over the field.

Many soldiers also wrote letters to their families telling them about the hardships of war.

There were 13,001 Iowans killed in the war; 3,540 died in battle and 8,498 from disease. Many of these men died in Confederate prison camps. Some Iowa soldiers were sent to Andersonville, Georgia, where the Confederates had a large prison camp. At Andersonville the prisoners had no shelter and little food, and many died from disease and exposure.

WOMEN IN THE WAR

Women in Iowa sewed clothing, even uniforms, for the soldiers. They knit sweaters, stockings, and mittens and made bandages. They also raised money to buy medicine and other supplies needed by the men and organized shipments to military camps. Sometimes women had to arrange for steamboats to carry the goods. These did not always reach the soldiers. Often food rotted before reaching the soldiers, and sometimes clothing was lost or thrown away.

Women making bullets to help the North fight the Civil War.

Hundreds of women took over farm work to support their families while their husbands served in the army. They planted crops, milked cows, and harvested grain. One woman supported her three children by buying nine cows. After milking the cows, she made butter, which she sold for sixty cents a pound. Many women became teachers. But even though they took on many different jobs, some women had trouble making enough money for their families.

While their husbands were away, wives wrote them many letters. Some of these letters have been saved, and they show that the lonely wives did their best to cheer up their husbands. Many women were lonely because they had just moved from Ohio or Pennsylvania and they did not know many people.

ANNIE WITTENMYER: A WOMAN IN WARTIME

Annie Wittenmyer in her later years, about 1880.

Most soldiers in the Civil War were men, but one Iowa woman was a different kind of soldier. Annie Wittenmyer probably did more than anyone else to provide care for the sick and wounded in the Union army. General Ulysses Grant, commander of the Union army, said, "No soldier on the firing line gave more heroic service than she did."

Annie Wittenmyer and her husband had moved to Keokuk in 1850, ten years before the Civil War began. At that time, Keokuk had no free public schools. Unhappy about that situation, Mrs. Wittenmyer hired a teacher and opened a free school for poor children. Along with other church women, she also provided meals and clothes for needy children. Mrs. Wittenmyer's husband died in those early years in Keokuk.

When the Civil War began, Mrs. Wittenmyer joined the Keokuk Aid Society, women who provided care for the wounded in army hospitals. In a hospital in Sedalia, Missouri, Mrs. Wittenmyer was helping her own brother when she saw what poor food the sick received. For breakfast, her brother was given a cup of cold coffee, a piece of greasy bacon, and a slice of bread.

Mrs. Wittenmyer decided that something had to be done. So she wrote letters to army officials, telling them about these miserable conditions, and she urged women throughout Iowa and the northern states to send food for the wounded. Soon she was put in charge of all hospital kitchens for the Union army. Mrs. Wittenmyer convinced other women to help her. Together they worked in the hospitals, making certain that the wounded received better meals than the army had been providing. They also collected bandages and blankets to make the sick more comfortable.

Some people criticized Mrs. Wittenmyer. They said that it was not a woman's place to be on the battlefield or to be taking care of wounded men. Mrs. Wittenmyer did not let these criticisms stop her. She still did her work and won the praise of President Lincoln.

Her work turned Annie Wittenmyer very much against the war when she saw the suffering that it created. She later wrote: "It was an inside view of hospitals that made me hate war as I had never known how to hate it before."

When the Civil War ended, Mrs. Wittenmyer saw that more things needed to be done. The orphan children of soldiers killed in the war needed homes. Mrs. Wittenmyer worked to provide for them. In Davenport, one children's home was named for her.

In 1898, Congress rewarded the unselfish work that Mrs. Wittenmyer had done. Her volunteer efforts had used up much of her own money, and so Congress voted to grant her a pension to live on.

> **It was an inside view of hospitals that made me hate war as I had never known how to hate it before.**
> —Annie Wittenmyer
> (Keokuk, 1865)

PEOPLE WHO OPPOSED THE WAR

Not everyone in Iowa supported the war. Some people believed that the South should be allowed to set up its own government. Others believed that all wars were wrong, including the Civil War. Still others feared that the war would end slavery, and then free blacks would come to Iowa and take jobs away from whites.

Most Iowans, however, supported the war and were very unhappy with those who did not. They called them Copperheads, after a poisonous snake, and pressured them to change their views.

Even though they faced criticism, many important people in Iowa remained Copperheads. One of these people was Charles Mason. A graduate from West Point Military Academy, Mason served as a member of Iowa's Territorial Supreme Court. George Wallace Jones, one of Iowa's first U.S. senators, was another who opposed the war. Jones had been friends at West Point with Jefferson Davis, the president of the Confederate States of America. Therefore people believed that Jones could not be trusted, and he was put in prison for a time. Jones insisted that he was loyal to the Union, but he believed the war was wrong. Sometimes family members did not support the same side in the war, and two of Jones's sons fought in the Confederate Army. After the war, Jones did not hold any more public offices.

Dennis Mahony, editor of a large newspaper, *The Dubuque Herald,* was also a Copperhead. Mahony wrote articles criticizing the federal government and also said that President Lincoln was wrong to start a war against the South. Lincoln did not like to be criticized and had Mahony and several others arrested. Federal marshals arrived in Dubuque in the middle of the night and took

> I will not do battle against the Southern people and rather than do so I will leave my own beloved Iowa.
> —George Jones (Iowa Senator, 1861)

106

Mahoney to prison in Washington, D.C. Even his wife could not find out why he had been arrested. Mahony was released several months later, but only after he had promised not to sue the U.S. government for his imprisonment.

Although most Iowans supported the war, it is important to know that not all people did so. American citizens have a right to express their views, even if those views are unpopular. In Iowa, people who opposed the war were courageous. They knew that their statements would make them unpopular and that other people would criticize them. Even so, they stood up for their beliefs.

POLITICS IN IOWA

The Civil War brought many changes in Iowa, some of them affecting the political parties. During the 1840s, most Iowans were Democrats. The problem was that Democrats in the South believed in slavery. But most Democrats who lived in the North opposed slavery. Because of these two views, the Democratic party obviously could not make all its members happy. In the 1850s, many Iowans left the Democratic party and joined a new group, the Republican party. Unlike the Democrats, the Republicans did not have many members in the South.

The Republican party did not want slavery to spread to states *outside* the South. But they were not trying to do away with slavery *in* the South. Iowans liked these views. They agreed that people who lived in the western states and territories should not be allowed to own slaves. In 1860 most Iowans voted for Abraham Lincoln, who was the first Republican candidate to become president. After the Civil War, Iowa became a strong Republican state.

State Historical Society, Culbertson Collection

President Abraham Lincoln.

FURTHER READING

Danbom, David B. " 'Dear Companion': Civil War Letters of a Story County Farmer." *The Annals of Iowa* 47, no. 6 (Fall 1984). Iowa City: State Historical Society of Iowa.

Nelson, Julie E., and Alan M. Schroder. "Iowa and the Civil War: A Military Review." *The Palimpsest* 63, no. 4 (July/August 1982). Iowa City: State Historical Society of Iowa.

Peterson, Richard W. "Tell the Boys I Die Happy." *The Palimpsest* 66, no. 6 (November/December 1985). Iowa City: State Historical Society of Iowa.

Wall, Jospeh F. "We Fight for the Land." In *Iowa: A Bicentennial History.* New York: W. W. Norton, 1978. Chapter 6.

Iowans were fortunate that no battles were fought in their state. Because of that, no homes or businesses were destroyed and Iowans could go on with their work immediately after the war. That was not true in the South, where people suffered for many years because of the destruction caused by the war.

After the war, Iowa grew rapidly. More and more people came to start new farms and businesses. They moved into northwest Iowa, the last part of the state to be settled, so that within a few years after the war, all of Iowa had been settled. Before long, four major railroads were completed across the state, which allowed even more new businesses.

Iowa also changed as a result of the war. Many Iowans switched from the Democratic to the Republican party. African Americans in Iowa were given more rights after the war. In 1868, black men were given the right to vote, and later they were allowed to serve in the state legislature. By 1875, black children were attending public schools. The state was growing in every way.

Settlers from Many Lands

Throughout Iowa's history, the state has attracted immigrants from all over the world—Europe, Africa, Asia, and South America. The first settlers wanted to buy land and become farmers. Later immigrants often found jobs in factories and stores. Because of our immigrant history, Iowa is home to people of many different backgrounds.

This chapter tells about many of the people who immigrated to Iowa. It describes some of their distinctive achievements. Although the chapter emphasizes the activities of the earliest immigrant groups, remember that the story of immigrants coming to Iowa continues to the present. Iowa still offers settlers the chance for a better life, just as it did many years ago.

PUSH AND PULL

People who came to Iowa in the 1800s had several reasons for immigrating. Historians use the term "push-pull factors" to describe them. Push factors were the reasons why people wanted to leave their homelands, and pull factors were the attractions of the country to which they were going. Most immigrants felt both. In Europe

> The greater part of the land in England is owned by the high aristocratic families.
> —English immigrant (1850)

109

few people owned land because land was expensive and most people could not afford it. But Europeans knew that land in the United States was cheap. This is an example of how the push-pull factors worked. The main reason that people moved to America in the 1800s was to become landowners. For the immigrants LAND was the magic word.

Other reasons that people left Europe were because of religious problems. They knew they could attend any church they wanted to in the United States, or even start a new one. Many people left Sweden in the mid-1800s because they disagreed with Lutheran authorities over the payment of church taxes. In 1847, about eight hundred people left Holland because they did not want to belong to the state church. In Iowa, Hollanders started the community of Pella, where they worshiped as they pleased.

Some families left Germany because they differed with their government over the harsh treatment given their sons when they were required to serve in the military.

Other families immigrated to Iowa because they wanted their children to have a better life. In Denmark in the 1800s, poor families often had to "hire out" their children. Hiring out meant that the children went to work for nearby farmers and business people. Boys gen-

A boatload of immigrants crossing the Atlantic Ocean on their way to America, around 1900.

State Historical Society

erally worked for dairy farmers and girls did housework for others. Sometimes children hired out as early as nine years of age. Once they left the family, the children usually continued to live away from home. Danish parents believed that in the United States they could better care for their children and keep them at home longer.

Letters Home

There [in America] I shall certainly meet with the same wickedness which troubles me here; yet I shall find also opportunity to work. There I shall certainly find the same, if not still greater, evidence of unbelief and superstition; but I shall also find a constitutional provision which does not bind my hands in the use of . . . the word of God. There I shall find no Minister of Public Worship, for the separation of Church and State is a fact.

(1846)

How different from Holland! In the land of our birth, branded and treated as a despised congregation, misunderstood by everyone, shoved aside, trampled upon and bruised; in the land of strangers . . . honored and treated as a costly gift of God to improve their country!
–Hendrik Peter Scholte
(Dutch immigrant, Pella, 1848)

Although we were very happy [in Sweden] . . . one is always trying to better one's condition and way of living. My father had friends and relatives in America who kept writing about the wonders of this new land. So, being an adventurous person, for many years he had been wanting to try his fortune in the new land of the free, which seemed to be a chance for prosperity, but mother was not of the same mind. She thought that it would be too much to give up her home and her friends. At last, after much persuasion, she was won over. I know that it must have been hard since she was not of the same nature as he, but she cut herself adrift from all ties, and started to get us ready for the long trip, which was to change our lives so much.

—John M. Stromstern
(Swedish immigrant, Corydon)

Departing from you dear father, was very hard on me . . . But oh, dear father, we did not leave to get away from you, as you know very well. It was for the purpose of going to a country where we, by working hard, could expect a better way of life than in Vriesland [a province in the Netherlands]. And we have not been disappointed . . . for if we remain healthy, within a few years we can start on our own farm, which would never have become a reality in Vriesland. . . . Considering everyone in his own trade, there is not one person who, by moving to America, does not earn more than a common laborer over there. If we had stayed in Vriesland very likely within a few years we would have been reduced to utter poverty.

—Sjoerd Aukes Sipma
(Dutch immigrant, Pella, 1848)

The greater part of the land in England is owned by the high aristocratic families. The population is still increasing while demand for labour is less because of the ever-increasing productions of mechanical power. The desire to emigrate to a place where every man may with little difficulty become an independent landowner, will increase.

—English immigrant (1850)

Every farm, especially in the southern part of Sweden, had as many tenants as was possible without encroaching too much on the best portion of the estate which was always kept by the owner himself. Each tenant was allowed a patch of ground from half an acre to ten or fifteen acres. The larger tenants paid their rent in money, the smaller in labor to the land owner. In a great many instances he had to labor every day in the year excluding Sundays and holidays, the tenant furnishing his own board. Where one had a large family to support it was slavery in a most aggravated form.

> —D. A. Peterson
> (Swedish immigrant, Casady's Corners)

As soon as Iowa opened for settlement in 1833, immigrants began to arrive and they continued to come in search of land for the rest of the nineteenth century. At first they came from northern Europe and the British Isles. Norwegians settled in northeastern Iowa, around Decorah. Some English settled in northwest Iowa. Dan-

KEY

SCANDINAVIAN (NORWEGIAN, SWEDISH, DANISH)

GERMAN (AMISH, AMANAS, SWISS AMISH, MENNONITE)

IRISH

ENGLISH

DUTCH

CZECH

SCOTTISH

WELSH

FRENCH (ICARIANS)

ITALIAN

INDIAN (MESQUAKIE)

AFRICAN AMERICAN

HUNGARIAN

Major ethnic groups in Iowa.

113

For many years he had been wanting to try his fortune in the new land of the free.
—John Stromstern (Corydon, 1860s)

ish people made a large settlement in southwestern Iowa. The Czechs from eastern Europe settled in eastern Iowa around Cedar Rapids. From the start, Iowa's immigrants took part in community life.

By 1900, the United States census showed that Iowa had about three hundred thousand people who had been born in foreign countries.

The largest foreign-born groups in Iowa in 1900

Germany	123,162	Denmark	17,102
Sweden	29,874	Canada	15,687
Ireland	28,321	Austria	13,118
Norway	25,634	Netherlands	9,388
England	21,027	Bohemia*	9,098

*Bohemia's figures are for 1905. Today we know this country as Czechoslovakia.

GERMAN IMMIGRANTS

German immigrants were the largest group to come to Iowa. They settled in every part of the state. Because they had reputations as good farmers, Iowa welcomed them. Germans also settled in towns and started businesses.

Marx and Anna Goettsch were German immigrants who came to Davenport in the 1870s. Marx had learned to make shoes in Germany, and in Davenport he opened a shoe shop. In the 1870s most people wore shoes made by local shoemakers. Within a few years, Marx and Anna made enough money from the shoe business to buy several houses, which they rented out.

The Goettsches spent most of their time with their family and other German Americans, with whom they spoke German. They were members of the Turner Society, a German-American organization. Every week they went to the Turner Hall, where they sang German

114

State Historical Society

The Turner Hall in Guttenburg where German-Americans met.

songs, discussed politics or social questions, and visited with other members. Each hall included a gym with exercise equipment and a small auditorium where visiting stage companies put on plays. The Turner slogan was "a sound mind in a sound body."

The Goettsches' experience is a good example of what happened to immigrants in the United States. The Goettsches wanted to live in America but they still thought of themselves as Germans. They could not forget their German identity and went on speaking German. The Goettsches were really trying to do two things. They were trying to keep their German ways and still become Americans.

Marx and Anna had five sons and one daughter. Unlike their parents, the Goettsch children did not think of themselves as Germans, but rather as Americans. They spoke German to their parents, but they spoke English in school and to their friends. The children liked the German food that their mother cooked, but they also liked American food. All five Goettsch sons went to college. One son became an engineer and two other sons became medical doctors. The daughter, however, did not even go to high school. Marx Goettsch believed that his daughter should go to work rather than go to school. So she worked for ten years as a seamstress in a Davenport store before she married.

If Marx and Anna Goettsch had stayed in Germany, their sons probably would not have had the education and the opportunities they had here in the United States.

Today, towns like Dubuque, Davenport, and other Mississippi River communities still have signs of German culture. There are three Turner halls in Davenport. Burlington has a church (now an art museum) that was built as the German-American Methodist Church. There are old breweries (places that make beer) started by German immigrants in Dubuque and Burlington.

SCANDINAVIAN IMMIGRANTS

Many people immigrated to Iowa from the Scandinavian countries of Sweden, Norway, and Denmark.

The Swedes

The first group to arrive were the Swedes, who created New Sweden in 1845. Led by Peter Cassel, the Swedes came to buy land and take up farming.

A few years later a second Swedish community was started in Boone County by accident. The group, consisting of forty-one people, was led by Anna Dalander. Mrs. Dalander had written to Peter Cassel asking him how to reach New Sweden. Knowing that the Dalander group would travel the last part of their journey on the Missis-

116

sippi, Cassel sent the following instructions:

> Come up the Mississippi River until you reach Iowa. Then follow the east side of the river that flows into the Mississippi.

What Peter Cassel did not realize was that there were two rivers close together in southeastern Iowa, the Des Moines and the Skunk. Mrs. Dalander's group discovered the two rivers and became confused. They chose to follow the Des Moines River, probably because it was the largest.

It was fall, and as they started their trek along the river, the Swedes worried about the coming winter. They were traveling with only a little food into a part of Iowa that had few settlers. After a time, the group arrived at Fort Des Moines, where the city of Des Moines is today. The soldiers reported that there was no settlement known as New Sweden in that area. With winter coming on, the soldiers urged the lost Swedes to turn back.

Certain that they were right, however, the group pushed on, following the river. Finally they reached the cabin of Thomas Gaston, the only white settler in the area. By then, Mrs. Dalander and her group had traveled over two hundred miles inland. The Swedes were lucky to find someone who had extra food that they could buy. They remained with Gaston through the winter, and in the spring they decided to settle in Boone County. They first named their community Swede's Point, but it was later changed to Madrid.

Norwegians and Danes

The second Scandinavian group to immigrate to Iowa was Norwegian. The first Norwegians settled in northeast Iowa, around the town of Decorah. Those who

> My father had friends and relatives in America who kept writing about the wonders of this new land.
> —John Stromstern (Corydon, 1860s)

117

Here we sat, Vilhelm and I, separate for the first time from relatives and friends, in a little log cabin far inland in America.
—Elizabeth Koren (Decorah, 1853)

arrived later found land farther west, along the northern edge of the state. Others settled in Story County, and today their descendants live in central Iowa around Story City and Huxley.

The Norwegians built a museum in Decorah called the Vesterheim, which means Western Home. Displays show how their ancestors lived in Norway and their early life in Decorah. Like other immigrants, the Norwegians brought along crafts from their homeland. One of these is a folk art called rosemaling, which involves painting flowers and colorful designs on bowls, cabinets, and other wooden items.

Iowa is also noted for its Danish settlers. The national Danish-American museum is being built in Elkhorn because so many people of Danish descent live in Shelby and Audubon counties.

CHRISTMAS IN IOWA
A GIFT FROM MANY LANDS

Christmas in America was not always the important holiday that it is today. In early New England, some people did not celebrate it at all, and as late as the 1870s, schoolchildren in Boston went to class on Christmas Day.

Many early Iowa pioneers celebrated the day only with a special meal. Kitturah Belknap, a young pioneer wife in southeastern Iowa in 1841, wrote her plans for the meal in her diary.

Firstly; for bread, nice light rolls; cake, doughnuts
For pie; pumpkin
Preserves; crab apples and wild plums
Sauce; dried apples
Meat, first round: roast spare ribs with sausage and mashed potatoes and plain gravy; second round:

118

chicken stewed with best of gravy; chicken stuffed and roasted in the Dutch oven by the fire, for I have never cooked a meal on a stove.

It was Kitturah's first year to cook Christmas dinner and on Christmas Day she wrote in her diary that "everything went off in good style." One of the older folks had even said that she "had no idea Kit could do so well."

Unlike the New Englanders, the Europeans who had moved to Iowa made Christmas a special holiday. People from Norway, Sweden, Denmark, and Germany usually had big Christmas celebrations and they brought their traditions along when they moved here.

Elizabeth Koren immigrated from Norway to northeastern Iowa with her husband, Vilhelm. He was a Lutheran minister who came to serve a group of Norwegians near Decorah. On Christmas Eve, 1853, her first Christmas in Iowa, she wrote in her diary:

This was a strange Christmas Even, indeed: so different from any I have know before. Here we sat, Vilhelm and I, separate for the first time from relatives and friends, in a little log cabin far inland in America. For supper, we had spareribs and coffee. As we sit here now, we get a little light from a lead dish in which there are tallow scraps and a little rag for a wick, placed on an overturned salt container.

An Iowa parlor decorated for Christmas about the time of World War I.

What a contrast between this evening and a year ago! I am happy and content that we are here in time for the Christmas festival—there is such joy over the pastor's coming—but it grieves me to think of Father and the others whom I miss, for the first time, on this Christmas Eve.

The Christmas tree was a tradition for many immigrants. The Freburg family, Swedish immigrants who lived near Pomeroy in northwest Iowa, tied ribbon bows on the branches, hung fruit and nuts on its boughs, or made small decorations for it. As in many homes, the Christmas tree was decorated in the parlor, a room used only for special occasions, and children were not allowed to see the tree until Christmas morning.

Waiting was so hard, recalled the Freburg's daughter Mildred, but when her parents opened the parlor door on Christmas morning, there it was! All over the tree were tiny lighted candles, giving off a flickering light, like little stars buried in the green branches. She remembered that beautiful tree for the rest of her life.

Not all families gave each other gifts at Christmas but usually there was one small gift for each child. It might be a doll, a spinning top, or a small whistle and was usually homemade. Some children received oranges as a special treat.

In time, gift-giving became common. Most people began celebrating Christmas, often borrowing customs from other groups. What we know today as Christmas is a mixture of many different traditions from the many different people who settled Iowa.

ITALIAN IMMIGRANTS

Until the 1880s, most immigrants who came to Iowa were "old immigrants" from northern Europe and the British Isles. Then immigration patterns began to change as more people arrived in America from southern and eastern Europe. Included among the "new immigrants" were people from Italy, Croatia (now in Yugoslavia), Hungary, Poland, Lithuania, and Russia. Most of the new immigrants settled in cities in the northeastern United States, where they went to work in factories and on construction projects. A small number, especially Italians, came to Iowa.

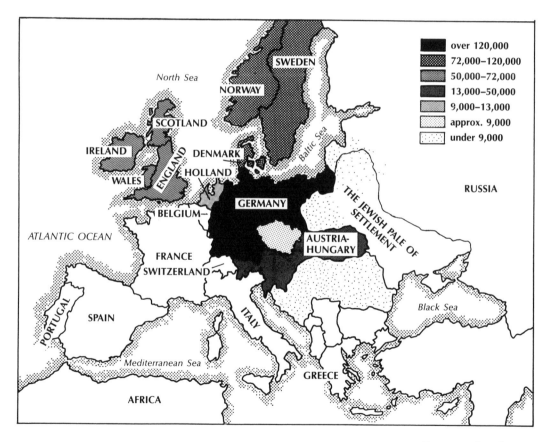

European immigrants to Iowa, 1820–1920.

Italians began settling in Iowa around 1900. Many settled in cities and towns rather than the countryside. They often found jobs in coal mines or on the railroads.

State Historical Society

Miners with their mules outside a coal mine in Webster County, 1890.

Coal mining played an important part in the lives of some Italian Americans. Although it was hard work and often dangerous, it did offer some advantages. Once they started working they were able to send money to family members in Italy. This was sometimes used to bring a brother or parent to the United States.

A number of Italian Americans lived in small communities located next to the coal mines, such as Granger and Lovilia. These were often referred to as coal camps. These communities usually consisted of about one hundred houses, a grade school, and a few businesses. When boys finished the eighth grade, they often went to work in the mines. Girls usually stayed home to help their mothers after they finished their schooling. Children growing up near the mines had little opportunity to go on to high school or find other work. Some continued to live in the mining community after they were married. When

122

the coal camps closed, many Italians moved to Iowa's major cities in search of other work.

After World War I, the United States government passed immigration laws that reduced the number of people who could come into the country. The new laws allowed only a few thousand eastern and southern Europeans to come into the United States during the 1920s.

AFRICAN AMERICANS IN IOWA

African Americans began migrating to Iowa in the mid-1800s, some to farms, others to towns. First a few slaves arrived with their masters and lived in the southeastern part of the state, just across the Missouri border. Before long, however, more African Americans headed north and settled in the Hawkeye state. By 1900, Iowa had 12,693 African-American people out of a total population of 2,231,853.

Before the Civil War, most Iowans did not think that

State Historical Society

A district Sunday school meeting of the African Methodist Episcopal Church in Waterloo, 1914.

blacks should be treated the same as whites. In fact, Iowans passed several laws that were intended to keep African Americans out of the state. In 1838 and 1840, Iowa legislators passed laws known as Iowa's Black Code. One law said that no black person could come into the state without a certificate of freedom proving that the black was not a runaway slave. Another law said blacks and whites could not marry. At that time, black men could not vote or serve in the state legislature and black children could not attend public schools.

After the Civil War, laws about African Americans changed in Iowa, as in many parts of the United States. Black men were given the right to vote and to serve in the Iowa state legislature. In the 1860s, an African-American barber and seller of wood to steamboats, Alexander Clark, had a twelve-year-old daughter, Susan, who wanted to attend public school in Muscatine. Clark filed several lawsuits challenging the fact that Susan had to go to a different school from the one white children attended. After three separate decisions by the Iowa Supreme Court, the law was changed so all children attended the same schools.

Even though African Americans won some rights, they still faced problems. Many restaurants would not serve them and some employers would not give them jobs. Most railroads in Iowa would hire black men only as waiters and porters, not as the better-paid engineers and conductors. Even with discrimination, however, blacks worked as deckhands on steamboats and as builders of railroads. Some opened up their own businesses, especially restaurants and barber shops. The largest number of African Americans worked as coal miners.

The first group of African-American mining families settled in Muchakinock. This was a coal camp in southern Mahaska County, operated by the Consolidation Coal Company. The population of Muchakinock was about one-third African American out of a total population of 3,500 people.

In 1900 many people moved from Muchakinock to Buxton, a larger coal camp. For a while there were more blacks than whites in Buxton. African Americans worked as coal miners, but many owned businesses or were professional people.

When Buxton closed down, many African Americans stayed in Iowa, but others moved out of the state. Like the Italians, those who stayed moved to Des Moines, Waterloo, and Cedar Rapids where they took jobs in factories, stores, meat-packing plants, and private homes. Others became prominent professionals—doctors, lawyers, teachers, newspaper editors, and clergymen.

African-American people soon discovered that living in Des Moines or Waterloo was very different from living in Buxton. In Buxton, everyone had been treated alike. In the other cities, African Americans often had trouble finding jobs and places to live. Sometimes they

> In Waterloo, I could not find a teaching job because they hired only white teachers.
> —Vaeletta Fields

Postal carriers in East Des Moines, 1896. Around 1900, blacks worked in many different occupations, such as delivering mail.

could not eat in certain restaurants or shop in certain stores. African-American people who moved to Waterloo sometimes were called terrible names because they were black.

One African-American woman, Vaeletta Fields, moved to Waterloo in the 1920s. She had graduated from the University of Iowa where she studied to be a teacher. In Waterloo she could not find a teaching job because they hired only white teachers. Mrs. Fields, whose husband was a lawyer, worked as a cleaning woman and as an elevator operator for many years. Gradually African-American people were able to get better jobs, but the changes came very slowly. Vaeletta Fields's mother, Mrs. Minnie London, was a schoolteacher in Buxton. Years later she wrote her memories of the town.

As I Remember

In the early spring of 1891 I went as a bride to what was once old Muchakinock, an Indian name that was derived from a nearby creek meaning, I was told, "hard to cross." It was a mining camp five or six miles from Oskaloosa, the county seat.

The camp, as it was called, had formerly been inhabited by white miners. When they went on a strike the Chicago and Northwestern Coal Company, who owned the mines, brought in colored [an old term for African-American] miners and their families from Staunton, Charlottesville, and other towns in Virginia. These colored men knew nothing of mining but were taught coal-mining by men hired by the Company. Besides the colored people there were also a goodly number of Swedes. . . . [Nine years later Minnie London moved to another mining town.]

The new camp was named Buxton, after the Superintendent of the Mines. . . . it attracted many people from various towns and cities of Illinois, Ohio, Kentucky, and Missouri, in fact from everywhere.

126

The London family at home in Buxton, around 1900, (*from left*) Minnie, Vaeletta, Hubert, and W. H. London. Minnie taught school in Buxton. Her husband owned a grocery store.

I am sure I am safe in saying that when the town, Buxton, was at its height, no other town in Iowa could boast so many professional and business people of our own group. Doctors, lawyers, teachers, druggists, pharmacists, undertakers, postmaster, Justice of the Peace, constables, clerks, members of the school board . . . were all there. . . .

Among business ventures in Buxton that stand out in my memory are: Lewis Reasby with his hamburger and hot dog stand across from the company store and in front of the Y.M.C.A. His comical manner of crying his wares would attract passers-by, who would stop and listen to him, then find themselves thrusting their hands into their pockets and saying, "A hot dog please."

Yes, Buxton had a newspaper too, namely the "Buxton Advocate." It was a weekly edited and owned by R. B. Montgomery.

The Y.M.C.A. was a large three-story structure built diagonally across from the company store. It was built expressly for the colored miners, and when they seemed reluctant to take advantage of the opportunity, the Supt. indicated that he would turn it over to the white people. Our people, after reconsideration, pledged cooperation. . . .

"Sharp End," I suppose, was the sudden

127

termination of the town to the south, and located in this area was a drug store owned and operated by Ike Hutchinson, whose wife Hattie was the registered pharmacist. . . .

Near the depot Anderson Perkins and Son operated a hotel and confectionery. They advertised good meals and first class service. Hotel rates $1.00 and $1.50. . . .

The [schools] were all well filled with pupils and often a teacher would have to instruct several grades. The grade work done in these schools compared favorably with any in the state. For instance, whenever pupils from these schools went to school in other places, I have been told by the teachers of other towns that they were always glad to get the Buxton children because of their thoroughness.

After several years the number of pupils to enter High School became greater so the School Board erected a large building east of the Fifth Street School maintaining two years of High School to begin with. They employed a Prof. Gilliam as Superintendent. After one year of occupancy it burned down just the Sunday before the beginning of the first semester of the second year. The cause of the loss was said to have been due to the construction of the building. It was never rebuilt so to other towns in the state High School pupils had to continue to go.

About 1921 many of the pioneers were destined to be moved to another coal field as the mines at Buxton were just about worked out. The new camp was called Haydock, still in Monroe County about eighteen miles distant over hills and valleys. Fewer still were willing to follow up the unstable life of a miner and so many continued to go to various cities. The camp had already been populated by many white miners and their families, mainly from Illinois, thus there were less colored people and very few business ventures.

— Minnie B. London

IMMIGRATION AND WORLD WAR I

When World War I began in Europe in 1914, the number of immigrants coming to the United States fell. Because of fighting between countries, ships were sunk and it was dangerous or impossible to travel from Europe to the United States. Some countries refused to let their young men leave, insisting that they serve in the army.

Before the war, a large number of European immigrants had worked in factories and plants. Once the war began and immigration was shut off, American business people had to look to other countries for workers. A company in Bettendorf, which made train equipment, began to bring in workers from Mexico. Mexicans also immigrated to other parts of Iowa.

Hispanic Immigrants

In 1910 there were only 590 Mexican Americans in Iowa, but by 1920 that number had risen to about 2,500. Some of these Spanish-speaking settlers worked in agriculture, while others found jobs in Iowa cities. For example, some Mexican Americans moved to West Des Moines where they worked in the railroad yards. Others made their homes in Mason City, Davenport, or Council Bluffs.

More recently, Mexican Americans have come to Iowa and other parts of the Midwest to work in meatpacking plants. They have settled both in larger communities, such as Sioux City, and in smaller towns, such as Columbus Junction. In 1990, 32,647 Hispanics resided in Iowa. Spanish is the second major language used in the state on an everyday basis. As the Latino community grows, Latin American music and food and fiestas have enriched Iowa's cultural life.

RECENT IMMIGRATION

The most recent immigrants to Iowa are refugees from Southeast Asia who began coming to our state in 1975. War had been going on in Southeast Asia for many years, and people who lived there suffered greatly. Thousands of Vietnamese, Cambodian, Laotian, and Hmong people left their homes, seeking refuge (a place they would be protected) from danger and from governments that they feared.

One group from Southeast Asia are the Tai Dam. Until the 1250s they had lived in China, after that in North Vietnam, and then in Laos. When Laos was taken over by the communists, the Tai Dam fled to Thailand and from there some of them came to Iowa. People here, especially Governor Robert Ray, helped the Tai Dam get settled. That meant helping them find homes and jobs and get their children started in school. In their first two

Vietnamese refugees in Des Moines, 1975. People from Southeast Asia are among Iowa's newest immigrants.

State Historical Society

decades in Iowa, the Tai Dam have repeated much of the experience of Iowa's other immigrant groups: they have worked hard, participated in community activities, and won a place in Iowa society. Tai Dam leaders are respected by other community leaders and consulted on such public matters as education and human services.

Like earlier immigrants, the Tai Dam families have brought along their crafts and culture. At different events in Des Moines they have presented native dances and prepared special food.

> **If we remain healthy, within a few years we can start our own farm, which would never have become a reality in Vriesland.**
> **—Sjoerd Sipma (Pella, 1848)**

All through the nineteenth and twentieth centuries people have immigrated to Iowa. They came here because of poor conditions in their homelands and because of the opportunities in the United States. Most immigrants wanted to buy land and become farmers, but others preferred to seek their fortunes in Iowa's cities and towns. Iowa's immigrant groups have had many different occupations.

Immigrants have made an important economic contribution to our state. They settled on the land to produce corn and pork and other things to sell. These sales brought money into the state. Immigrants who settled in cities and towns did their part to help the state develop and become more prosperous.

All of us except American Indians are descendants of immigrants. Some of our great-grandparents or great-great-grandparents came from Europe. Ancestors of other Iowans came from Africa or Southeast Asia. Because most of our country is made up of descendants of immigrants, we are much like other states. Each ethnic group has contributed something different to our culture—words, crafts, or holidays. Our rich cultural heritage is a gift from the many immigrants who settled here.

FURTHER READING

Bonney, Margaret, ed. "Immigrants," *The Goldfinch* 3, no. 2 (November 1981). Iowa City: State Historical Society of Iowa.

Cooper, Arnie. "A Stony Road: Black Education in Iowa, 1838–1860." *The Annals of Iowa* 48, nos. 3, 4 (Winter/Spring 1986). Iowa City: State Historical Society of Iowa.

Schwieder, Dorothy. *Black Diamonds.* Ames: Iowa State University Press, 1983.

Swierenga, Robert P. "A Dutch Immigrant's View of Frontier Iowa." In *Patterns and Perspectives in Iowa History,* Dorothy Schwieder, ed. Ames: Iowa State University Press, 1973.

Providing a Government

As Americans began settling on lands west of the Mississippi River, they needed to set up a government. There had to be laws and officers to enforce them. The settlers wanted to send representatives to speak for them in Congress. They also needed help on projects at home, like building roads and setting up schools. Fortunately, the national government had provided settlers with a way to do this, and Iowa pioneers knew that some day their new state would have the same rights as the older states.

THE IOWA TERRITORY

When the United States won its freedom from Great Britain, there were thirteen original states. West of these states, the land was controlled by the national government. At first, there were so few American citizens living in the western regions that they did not need much government.

Before a new region became a state, it was first a district and then a territory. A district had very few people. The president of the United States appointed a dis-

132

trict governor, and the army helped to keep order. As more American settlers arrived, the district became a territory. A territory also had a governor appointed by the president. The settlers in a territory were permitted to elect their own legislature to make laws for the new region. However, territories had no representatives in Congress in Washington. As still more people moved in, the territory became a state and elected its own governor and legislature. It also elected representatives to Congress to make laws for the entire nation.

Iowa went through these steps to become a state. When the United States bought Louisiana from France in 1803, Iowa was made part of a large district west of the Mississippi. In 1834, Iowa became part of the Michigan Territory, which included what is today Michigan, Wisconsin, Minnesota, Iowa, and parts of the Dakotas. When Michigan became a state in 1836, the rest became the Wisconsin Territory.

People who settled west of the Mississippi wanted a government of their own. In 1838, Congress created the Iowa Territory out of the western part of the Wisconsin Territory. The Iowa Territory stretched north from the Missouri border across Iowa, southern Minnesota, and into North and South Dakota. In 1838, there were 22,859 people in the Iowa Territory. Most lived near the Mississippi River.

President Martin Van Buren appointed Robert Lucas to be the first governor of the Iowa Territory. Lucas had already been governor of Ohio for four years. In the summer of 1838, he left his family in Ohio and took a steamboat down the Ohio River. His wife was unwilling to leave their pleasant home in Ohio for the Iowa frontier. She did not come until two years later. Lucas's 14-year-old son, Edward, followed his father to Iowa in 1839. Edward rode horseback all the way from Ohio and spent only $23.37½ cents on the trip.

A large crowd greeted the new governor the morning his steamboat pulled up to the dock in Burlington. Governor Lucas lost no time in getting to work. That very afternoon, he set a date for the election of the territorial legislature. It was also the governor's job to select a city to be the capital of the new territory. Lucas visited Dubuque and Davenport and considered them as possible sites. In the end he chose Burlington and set up his office there.

Robert Lucas, the first governor of the Iowa Territory.

The legislature of the new territory had two parts, the Council and the House of Representatives. The Council had thirteen members whose terms lasted for two years. The House of Representatives had twenty-six members, each of whom served for one year. The legislature made laws for the new territory, but each law had to be approved by the governor.

The first legislature met in Burlington. Because there had been no time to build a hall, they met through the week in the Old Zion Methodist Church. To gain more room, the Council later moved to St. Paul's Catholic Church while the House of Representatives stayed in Old Zion.

Old Zion Church in Burlington, where Iowa's first legislature met, 1838–1841.

The legislature did not build its own meeting hall in Burlington because it did not expect the capital to stay there. Settlers were moving beyond the Mississippi, and Burlington was too far southeast to be an easy place to reach. The legislature decided to move west to Johnson County and directed Governor Lucas to select the exact spot for the new capital. They named the new town "Iowa City" even before they decided where it would be located. In 1839, two men rode horseback up the Iowa River until they found a beautiful site with hills gently sloping down to the water's edge. This became the site of the new capital, Iowa City. (The *city* where the government is located is called the capit*al*. The *building* for the legislature and officials is called the capit*ol*—"o" as in dome.)

The graceful stone Old Capitol in Iowa City is the work of John Francis Rague, the architect who also designed the Illinois capitol. It was ready for use in 1842 and remained the seat of Iowa government for fifteen years. Today Old Capitol is in the center of the University of Iowa campus.

State Historical Society

IOWA BECOMES A STATE

Governor Lucas wanted Iowa to become a state as soon as possible, but most of the early settlers wanted to wait until there were more people. The population was growing rapidly, however. In 1844, Iowa voters decided to begin the steps to become a state.

The first step was to draw up a state constitution. This is the basic law of the state and tells how the state government will be set up. It explains the powers and duties of each part of the state government.

A group met in Iowa City and wrote a constitution. One of their jobs was to recommend what the boundaries of the new state should be. They approved borders that would have made Iowa bigger than it is today. The northern border extended north to the present-day cities of Minneapolis and St. Paul. If that border had been approved, people who are living in southern Minnesota today would be Iowans.

This constitution had to be approved by both the Congress in Washington, and by the voters in Iowa. Congress approved the basic plan but changed the borders of the state. Instead of the Missouri River for a western border, Congress suggested a line about eighty miles to the east. If that border had been approved, people who are living in western Iowa today would be Nebraskans.

Iowa voters did not like the changes and refused to accept the borders Congress wanted. A new plan was made that created the borders we know today. Both Congress and the people of Iowa approved it. On December 28, 1846, President James K. Polk signed the law making Iowa the twenty-ninth state.

> Iowa—our eyes have been permitted to behold only the beginning of her glory.
> —Gov. Samuel Kirkwood (inscription on the Iowa Capitol)

Events that led to Iowa's statehood

1803	Louisiana is purchased from France.
1834	Iowa becomes part of Michigan Territory.
1836	Iowa becomes part of Wisconsin Territory.
1838	Iowa Territory is established.
1846	Iowa becomes a state.

In the first years of statehood, the population grew quickly. Reports of the fertile soil attracted thousands of new settlers. In 1846, Iowa's population was 96,000. In the next four years, it rose to 192,000. The next six years saw fantastic growth. By 1856, there were 518,000 Iowans. Most came in covered wagons or by steamboat. A few even arrived on the newly built railroad lines.

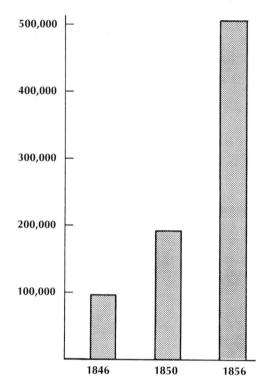

Iowa's population growth in the first ten years of statehood.

SETTING UP COUNTIES

To handle the needs of the new arrivals, the state created counties. Most counties are squares of land about twenty-four miles on each side. County government is close to the people. Local officials do things that people need more often or more quickly than a state government could provide.

For example, early settlers needed law officers close by. A county officer records the purchase and sale of land. Setting up schools, collecting taxes, providing places for people to vote on election day—these are things that counties were set up to do. It is easier for

138

people when these services are offered closer to home.

At first, when there were only pioneer families, the territory was divided into just two counties. The northern county was called Du Buque. The southern one was De Moine. These giant counties were soon divided into smaller parts.

By the time Iowa became a state in 1846, there were forty-four counties covering the eastern half of the state. In 1851, as more and more settlers were moving west, the legislature created forty-five new counties all at once. Today, Iowa is divided into ninety-nine counties.

In every county, there is a courthouse where county officials work. This is where the judge hears cases in the courtroom. Many people go to the courthouse to buy license plates for their cars and to pay their taxes. Older Iowa courthouses are often grand buildings of brick or stone.

The town where the courthouse is located is called the county seat. Towns in early Iowa competed to be the county seat because the county seat usually became the largest and most important town in the county.

> Our liberties we prize and our rights we will maintain.
> —Iowa state motto

A NEW CONSTITUTION

As the state continued to grow, some changes seemed necessary. In 1857, delegates met in Iowa City to write a new constitution for the state. In many ways, it was like the one adopted in 1846, but there were some important changes. The first constitution had prohibited (forbidden) banks, because early settlers feared that banks would not handle their money safely. The 1857 constitution allowed banks to operate in Iowa.

Another change was that the capital of the state was moved from Iowa City in the east to Des Moines, which

We the people of the state of Iowa, grateful to the Supreme Being for the blessings hitherto enjoyed . . . do ordain and establish a free and independent government, by the name of the State of Iowa.
—Preamble to the Iowa Constitution (1857)

Where Law ends, tyranny begins.
—Sir William Pitt (inscription on the Iowa Capitol)

was in the middle of the state. With people settling in western Iowa, Des Moines was easier for western citizens to reach.

The 1857 constitution is still the basic law of Iowa although there have been some changes over the years. A change in the constitution is called an amendment. The constitution set up a state legislature to make laws. There are two parts of the legislature, the Senate and the House of Representatives. Today, senators are elected for four-year terms and representatives for two-year terms.

To pass a new law, the House and Senate must each approve it. Then they send it to the governor. If the governor approves and signs it, it becomes a law. If the governor does not think it is a good idea, he vetoes (refuses to approve) it and it goes back to the legislature. Then, if two-thirds of both the House and the Senate still vote "Yes," it becomes a new law for the state, even if the governor does not agree.

Under the 1857 constitution, the governor was elected every two years. In 1972, the constitution was changed to give the governor a four-year term. The governor appoints many officials and supervises their activities. Some of his appointments to top jobs must be approved by the Senate also.

The constitution also set up judges and courts. The highest court in the state is the Iowa Supreme Court. The 1857 constitution required the people to elect judges in the same way they elected legislators and the governor. For over one hundred years, people who wanted to be a judge ran against each other in elections. Today, judges are appointed by the governor and approved by the Senate. But every ten years, the voters decide whether to keep a judge in office or not. If they decide to remove the judge, the governor appoints a new one.

140

Electing people to serve as government officials is important. A person whose name is on the ballot for people to choose in an election is called a candidate. Normally, there are at least two candidates running in an election. Voters must choose which one they want to be the government official. The candidate with the most votes wins.

The Iowa constitution sets up rules for who can vote in elections. In most cases, anyone who is eighteen years

WHO SHALL VOTE?

Every white male citizen of the United States, of the age twenty one years . . . shall be entitled to vote at all elections. [No blacks and no women can vote.]
—Article I, Section II, Iowa Constitution (1857)

Every male citizen of the United States, of the age twenty one years . . . shall be entitled to vote at all elections. [All men over twenty-one but no women can vote.]
—amendment to the Iowa Constitution (1868)

The right of citizens of the United States to vote shall not be denied or abridged by the United States or by any State on account of sex. [Both men and women over twenty-one can vote.]
—amendment to the United States Constitution (1920)

The right of citizens of the United States, who are eighteen years of age or older, to vote shall not be denied or abridged by the United States or by any State on account of age. [Men and women over eighteen can vote.]
—amendment to the United States Constitution (1971)

old and has lived in Iowa for ten days before the election can vote. To make sure that no one else votes, a county official keeps a list of all the people who meet the requirements. This is called the voter registration list. Iowans must register to make sure their names are on the list. When someone votes, an official puts a mark by that name. This way, no one can vote twice, and only registered voters get to vote. The place where people vote is called a polling place, or the polls. On election day, many polling places are set up in schools or churches or other central places to make it easy to vote.

POLITICAL PARTIES

Political parties are organizations that help select candidates to run for office and help them get elected. Through most of Iowa's history, the two most important

HAROLD HUGHES

Harold Hughes of Ida Grove was elected governor of Iowa three times. In 1968, he became a U.S. senator, where he played a role in national affairs.

Hughes became famous for the personal help ·he gave other people. As a young man, he had had a problem—he drank too much alcohol and could not seem to stop. After a hard struggle, he finally gave up alcohol and began to help others with their drinking problems. Because of this, he earned the respect of many people.

Hughes was also active in the Methodist Church. When he was in Washington, he often met for prayer with other politicians and sometimes preached sermons on what he believed. When his term in the Senate was finished, he did not run for re-election. He quit so that he could spend more time in his religious work.

parties have been the Republicans and the Democrats. After the Civil War, the Republican party was stronger than the Democratic party. In most elections, more Iowans voted for Republican candidates than for Democratic ones. In the 1930s, when many people were having a hard time, some Republicans became Democrats.

After World War II, the Democrats began winning elections. In 1956, Iowans elected a Democrat to be governor, and a Democrat was also elected to be one of Iowa's representatives in Congress. Another Democrat, Harold Hughes, became governor in 1962. Hughes led the Democratic party in Iowa for many years. His farsighted changes made the office of governor more powerful and gave Iowa a government that has worked well.

In 1968, a Republican named Robert Ray was elected governor. Ray had grown up in Des Moines and attended Drake University where he studied to become a

ROBERT RAY

Robert Ray served as Iowa's governor for five terms, longer than any governor before him.

Like Hughes, Governor Ray was also active in his church. For many years, Ray taught Sunday school in the Christian Church (Disciples). In the 1970s, he became concerned about the people of Southeast Asia. The war there had left many without homes, living in crowded camps with hunger and disease. Ray helped some of them move to Iowa. He urged church groups and others to assist homeless families. These groups helped them to find places to live, to learn English, and to get jobs. Soon, many Iowa towns included a few families from Vietnam or other Asian countries. These people joined the many other immigrant groups who had come to Iowa for a better life.

State Historical Society

lawyer. In his many years as governor the popular Ray continued the work of modernizing the government. The work of these two men, Hughes and Ray, helped to give Iowa good, fair, and open government.

Today both the Republican and Democratic parties are strong. Neither party always wins. Many Iowans vote for some Republican candidates and some Demo-

VOTES FOR WOMEN — FINALLY

Carrie Chapman Catt, the first woman to be school superintendent in Mason City, was a national leader in the efforts to obtain voting rights for women.

When Iowa became a state in 1846 women were not allowed to vote anywhere in the United States. Only men could choose public officials. At the time, many people thought that women were not as intelligent as men. Girls were not given as much education because it was thought they could not learn difficult subjects. Boys needed education. Husbands made the important decisions for their families, and on election day they decided which candidates would be the best officials.

In 1848, a group met in the small town of Seneca Falls, New York, to discuss the rights of women. Most were women, but there were some men. They wanted more education for women and women's suffrage (the right to vote). When the story was reported in the newspaper, people laughed at the idea of votes for women.

After the Civil War, there was more discussion of women's rights. In the early 1870s, the Iowa legislature debated the question. Some legislators thought that women should be able to vote, but most disagreed and refused to change the law. Through the next fifty years, some Iowans worked for this fundamental right.

Nearly everyone agreed that a woman's chief interest should be taking care of her home and family, but they were divided on whether women needed to vote. Some argued that if women were involved in politics

144

cratic candidates in the same election.

An interesting development in the 1970s and 1980s was the number of women running for political offices. In 1970, Minnette Doderer, a legislator from Iowa City, was nominated for lieutenant governor by the Democrats. In 1982 Roxanne Conlin became the Democratic candidate

they would neglect their families. They argued that women did not know enough about public affairs to vote sensibly. They feared that husbands and wives would argue about politics. Many thought that the nation would not have good leaders if women voted.

Others argued that women, like men, were citizens and deserved the right to vote. They pointed out that men could vote whether they knew anything about the candidates or not. Some expected *better* officials if women voted. Women would demand good schools for their children and might be able to force saloons to close.

In 1916, Iowa voters (only men, of course) were asked to decide whether women should be allowed to vote. The women's suffrage organization campaigned hard to urge Iowa voters to support votes for women. The election was close, but more men voted against the change, and women were still denied the right to vote.

During World War I, women worked hard to support the war effort. Many took jobs that men normally did—in factories, on farms, and even in the army. They proved that the old ideas about women only being able to work in the home were nonsense.

Finally in 1920, women all across the country were granted the right to vote. The United States Constitution, the highest law of the land, was changed to say that women could not be prevented from voting. Nearly seventy-five years after the Seneca Falls convention, women finally won this fundamental right.

> Iowa—the affections of her people like the rivers of her borders flow on to an inseparable union.
> —Enoch Eastman (inscription on the Iowa Capitol)

FURTHER READING

Bonney, Margaret, ed. "Government for Iowa." *The Goldfinch.* (Spring 1976). Iowa City: State Historical Society of Iowa.

———, ed. "The Shape of the State." *The Goldfinch* 4, no. 3 (February 1983). Iowa City: State Historical Society of Iowa.

———, ed. "Capitals and Capitols." *The Goldfinch* 5, no. 4 (April 1984). Iowa City: State Historical Society of Iowa.

Noun, Louise R. *Strong-Minded Women.* Ames: Iowa State University Press, 1969.

for governor. Both lost in the November elections, but they helped open up politics to other women candidates. Mary Jane O'Dell, a Republican, was elected secretary of state in 1982. In 1986, two women ran for lieutenant governor. Democrat Jo Ann Zimmerman won. In 1990 Republican Joy Corning was elected to the post.

In 1986, the first woman was appointed to the Iowa Supreme Court. Linda K. Neuman from Davenport was chosen by the governor to serve as one of the nine judges who make decisions on important cases.

Iowa plays a very important role in helping the United States select a president. Every four years, each political party chooses its candidate at a national convention. Every state sends representatives called delegates to the convention. To choose the delegates from Iowa, voters all over the state attend a political party meeting (a caucus) in their neighborhood. At the neighborhood caucus, they choose delegates to attend a county convention. From the county, delegates go to the state convention and then to the national convention, where each party's candidate for president is finally selected.

Because Iowa is the first state to begin choosing its delegates, presidential candidates all come to Iowa to get publicity. TV and newspaper reporters flock to the state to find out what Iowa voters are thinking. Many reporters are surprised to discover that most Iowans do not live on farms. They tell the nation that Iowa has excellent schools. They report that Iowans are friendly and take seriously their duty to be active in choosing candidates. Iowans like the attention that their caucuses get and want them to remain the first in the nation.

Reporters also say that Iowans take seriously the motto that flies on the state flag: "Our liberties we prize and our rights we will maintain."

146

10 Schools for a New State

As soon as they arrived in Iowa, pioneers began building schools. They felt strongly that their children needed to read and write to be good citizens. Soon after building schools, they built colleges as well. Today, as then, Iowans believe in good education.

THE PURITAN INFLUENCE

The Puritans, who came to New England from England in 1630, strongly believed in education. First, they thought that everyone must read the Bible, which they held to be the word of God. They also believed that learning to read made people more willing to work. Not working was viewed as being lazy, and to the Puritans, laziness was a sin.

To make certain that their children learned to read and therefore would work hard, the Puritans quickly set up grammar schools, which were much like our elementary schools. With so many grammar schools (and so many churches), the Puritans needed a place to train both teachers and preachers. Within six years they also

147

created Harvard College. Several generations later, the descendants of the Puritans began to move west. Everywhere these people went, they set up schools.

SETTING UP A SCHOOL SYSTEM

The first settlers in Iowa shared the early Puritans' views on education. Right away they took time to create schools and hire teachers. Often that was hard to do because early Iowans had little money and they were busy building homes and planting crops.

The first schools were subscription schools. Parents paid the teacher directly for the children they had in school. A family with four children paid more than a family that had two children in school.

State Historical Society

Birtha, Rudolph, and Arthur Stille set out for school near Nashua. Until the 1920s many Iowa children walked to country schools.

Later, schools were supported by the sale or rent of land. In 1785, the federal government had passed the Land Ordinance Act, which provided one section out of each township of thirty-six sections to support a school in that township. When Iowans discovered that they needed more money for schools, they started a property tax. This was a tax on homes, businesses, or farmland to pay for schools and for teachers' salaries.

As in other states, each town or township in Iowa became a school district. The district was controlled by an elected school board. The school board hired teachers, paid their salaries, planned new buildings, and provided for upkeep. School boards were made up of local people, often parents. Iowans, like most Americans, feel strongly that education should be controlled by people in that community.

The state government also became involved in education. Soon after the first schools opened, Iowans created a state department of education, under a state superintendent, to set up rules for Iowa schools to follow. This office decided what training teachers should have and what courses students should study. For many years, Iowa also had county school officials, who supervised all the teachers in the county and who organized short courses intended to help the teachers improve their teaching skills. They also made certain that all students were studying the proper courses.

THE FIRST SCHOOLS

Iowans built their first school in 1830, and Berryman Jennings was the first teacher. Jennings came from Kentucky to teach in a log cabin in Lee County. He had been hired by an early settler, Dr. Isaac Galland, and his first term lasted only three months.

Jennings had come to Iowa because he wanted to become a physician. In exchange for a room and board (meals) and being allowed to study Dr. Galland's medical books, Jennings promised to teach school. In the 1830s many doctors learned medicine not by going to college, but by reading books on their own.

Like the Galland school, early Iowa schools were often plain and simple log cabins. The cabins usually had benches along two walls. Boys sat on one bench and girls sat on the other. In most schools children were not divided into grades. Instead, children worked at their own speed. When a child had finished a set of books and problems, then she or he moved on to the next set. After reading all the books in the school, a child was usually ready to graduate.

At each school there was a recitation bench at the front of the room. Both parents and teachers believed that children learned best by memorizing, so students spent hours learning poems, short stories, and public speeches by heart. Then they sat on the bench to recite (speak) their lessons.

The blackboard was usually a wooden board painted black, and children used white limestone for chalk. To erase the blackboard, they used sheepskin erasers. Pupils had to bring their own textbooks to schools. If parents did not have enough money to buy books, children had to do without. Or they might use medical books, Bibles, or calendars for reading material.

A grade school at Agency in 1888.

State Historical Society

Iowa's early teachers were not paid much money for their work, usually only twenty or thirty dollars a month. Parents sometimes paid teachers by giving them room and board. The teacher would stay with each family for several weeks. The teachers stayed longest at the homes that had most children in school. At other times, parents paid teachers with butter, chickens, or other food.

Most schools hired a teacher for a three-month term—fall, winter, or spring. More pupils attended school during the winter term, including boys eighteen or nineteen years old. In the spring and fall, the older boys stayed out of school to help their fathers with farm work. Because of the presence of the older students, school boards felt that women teachers could not control the students, so a male teacher was often hired for the winter term.

All teachers sometimes had trouble. One early teacher wrote that it took him a week to settle his pupils down. Sometimes, because of misbehavior, he lined all his male students up along the wall and whipped everyone with a strap. Lon Chapin, who grew up in western Iowa, wrote this account of his school days in the 1880s.

He [the teacher] used to call up a lot of us at a time, and it was a big lot, too, reaching clear across the end of the room. Then came the order "remove your coats." He always started at the west end of the line and used a riding whip that a cowboy could call a quirt. We soon learned that the first 2 or 3 at the West end of the line got much the worst of it, we made an agreement that we would take turns as to who the first three should be. And it wasn't just an occasional round-up but every day and often several times a day. One day I achieved six, a record. And I was quite apt to boast of it.

151

Class Schedule 1870

9:00 A.M.	Opening Exercises
	Lord's Prayer
	Patriotic Poems and
	Axioms
9:15 A.M.	Roll
9:20 A.M.	Reading
9:40 A.M.	Mental Arithmetic
10:10 A.M.	Geography and Mapping
10:35 A.M.	Recess
10:50 A.M.	Written Arithmetic
11:15 A.M.	History and Our Constitution
11:45 A.M.	Meal Break and Recess
1:30 P.M.	Reading
2:00 P.M.	Physical Geography
2:30 P.M.	Grammar
3:15 P.M.	Blackboard Exercise
3:30 P.M.	Recess for Day

As Iowa's population grew, its schools improved. There was more money to build schoolhouses and to hire teachers. After 1900, school boards provided textbooks instead of having students bring their own. The most popular reading books were a series written by William McGuffey. *McGuffey's Reader*s included many different tales, each with a moral. A moral is a lesson in a story that points out the right way to behave. It is often summed up in a short saying at the end. The stories included the morals that children should obey their parents, honor their country and respect the flag, and be honest and work hard. There were verses with morals, too.

"Once or twice though you should fail,
Try, Try, Again;
If you would at last prevail,
Try, Try, Again;
If we strive, 'tis no disgrace,
Though we may not win the race;
What should you do in that case?
Try, Try, Again!

Many stories warned students that using tobacco was a dirty, wasteful habit. *McGuffey's Readers* also stressed the bad effects of alcohol. A verse about birds showed the advantages of not drinking.

Why do they twitter and sing, do you think?
Because they've had nothing but water to drink.

Parents agreed with McGuffey that children should be taught not to smoke or use alcohol. They also thought that the teachers themselves should provide good examples for the students. School boards could fire teachers who did not dress and behave as they were told. One teacher's contract included the following rules.

The teacher should not go out with any man except her brothers or father.

The teacher should not dress in bright colors.

The teacher should not use face powder or paint her lips.

The teacher should not loiter [stand around] in an ice cream parlor.

Another contract said women teachers must wear at least three petticoats under their skirts.

Every spring, the eighth graders took tests to see if they would graduate. If they passed, they then went to the county seat for a large graduation for all eighth graders in the county. This was an important time in a young person's life.

Many parents believed that an eighth grade education was enough for their children. If they could read, write, and do some arithmetic, young people did not need to attend high school. Most young Iowans did not attend high school until the 1920s.

Tobacco is a filthy weed That from the Devil does proceed. It drains your purse, It burns your clothes, And makes a chimney of your nose.
— Warning to schoolchildren (1800s)

153

Before there were many public high schools in Iowa, some young people went to private academies. These schools were set up and run by churches. Denmark, a small town in southeastern Iowa, was one of the first to have an academy. It was opened by the Congregational Church in 1843, and students came from all over Iowa and surrounding states. At the Denmark Academy boys and girls attended separate classes. Students studied the Bible and regular subjects like English and history. They also attended church regularly. Teachers at the Academy supervised the students closely, making certain that they did not dance or play cards. By the 1920s high schools had replaced academies and there were very few left in Iowa.

Denmark Academy in 1905.

State Historical Society

Tipton opened the first high school in the state in 1856. Others followed slowly because Iowans thought that grade schools were more important. At first, one high school in each county was enough. However, people began to see that more would be needed, especially in the larger towns and cities. By the 1920s, all of Iowa's cities and most towns had high schools and most students were going on beyond the eighth grade.

Milton High School graduation class of 1908.

COLLEGES AND UNIVERSITIES

Iowans began to set up colleges and universities in the mid-1800s. Not everyone wanted or needed a college education, but physicians and teachers did. Iowans also needed educated people to serve in state government. Most people believed that a high level of education would benefit everyone within the state.

155

By 1900, most religious groups ran at least one college in Iowa. Churches wanted students to get religious training as well as a good education. The Methodist Church had five colleges, one in almost every part of the state. The Catholic Church was the other leader, setting up separate schools for men and women.

The state government also set up colleges and universities in the nineteenth century. They were called public schools because they were set up and run with tax (public) money. The first one, the University of Iowa, held its first classes in Iowa City in 1855. It was established to train physicians, lawyers, and other professional people.

The next state school to open was Iowa Agricultural College, which later became Iowa State College and today is Iowa State University. Iowa State College was different in many ways from the University of Iowa. First, Iowa State was a land-grant school, meaning the federal government gave land to help start the school. In the nineteenth century, the federal government wanted some schools to teach agricultural and technical courses. To make certain that this happened, they gave land to states that were willing to set up such institutions. Iowa received 204,000 acres of land (located mostly in northwestern Iowa) to help start the college, which opened for classes in 1869. The state then used the money from the sale or rental of this land to operate the college.

At first Iowa State College was set up as a practical school where the students did "manual training" (physical work). This involved farm work for young men and cooking and cleaning for young women. Students were paid for their work—at ten cents per hour. After a few years, however, both parents and college officials decided that students were only doing the same work that they had done at home. So the college did away with manual training.

156

By the 1870s, people had become critical of the public schools, saying that teachers needed more training. So the state set up the Iowa State Normal School at Cedar Falls (later called the University of Northern Iowa).

Through the years Iowa's three state-supported universities have greatly expanded. Together, the schools prepare students to work in all occupations and professions. People who have graduated from Iowa's three universities live and work all over the world.

By 1910, Iowa had three state schools for higher learning. This is the Iowa teachers' college (now the University of Northern Iowa).

CHANGES IN OUR SCHOOLS

At first, children in Iowa did not have to attend school. Until the 1890s, most of the children who went to school attended only a few months each year. But in 1902, Iowa passed a law requiring all children between the ages of seven and sixteen to attend school.

An important change has been school consolidation (joining together), which started in northern Iowa where there were many small rural schools. By 1910, a few country schools had only one pupil. Parents and state officials believed that consolidation would lead to better schools. Larger schools could offer higher pay for teachers, more courses, and better buildings.

In 1897, children from country schools in Buffalo Township (Winnebago County) were bused into town as part of the first school consolidation in Iowa. They rode in six horse-drawn wagons called hacks. By 1921, over four hundred schools had consolidated. The move to consolidate stopped during the Depression of the 1930s but resumed again in 1945. Today, there are no one-room country schools left in Iowa. Instead, yellow school buses move through the countryside, carrying children to and from consolidated schools.

158

The first school buses at Huron School in 1919. In the early twentieth century children began riding to school in buses.

CHAUTAUQUA

Chautauqua Week (pronounced Sha TALK wa) was once the highlight of the Iowa summer. For a whole week traveling speakers, actors, and musicians came to town bringing learning and fun. They performed in a large tent, where the audience sat on benches or chairs. Often it was the best entertainment Iowans would see all year.

The word "Chautauqua" came from Lake Chautauqua in New York where in 1874 church leaders began a summer camp to train Sunday school teachers. They had music and speakers on many different subjects. Soon thousands of people were attending these classes each summer, and so Chautauqua leaders put the show "on the road." Chautauqua companies traveled throughout the country, presenting a week of programs in many cities and towns. Local committees promoted the event, sold tickets, and provided a place where the big tent could be set up.

When the big week arrived, many families, including some from nearby farms, camped by the Chautauqua tent for the entire time. It was their summer vacation. Some towns made special parks for the Chautauqua to be held, fixing up water faucets, restrooms, and camping facilities.

In the morning, the performers presented programs for children—a storyteller, or someone who led games. Next came lectures for mothers on raising children, or on health, or on art projects. In the evening, there might be a concert, a religious talk, a lecture by a famous politician, or a traveler to tell about a faraway land. Each year, a company of actors toured with the Chautauqua, performing different plays, sometimes comedies. Most of the programs were educational or religious. On Sunday, an outstanding minister preached a sermon. The Chautauqua was usually supported by all the churches in town.

Chautauquas remained active from 1900 to the

Iowans gathered in a tent at Lake City for a Chautauqua program.

160

1930s. In the later years, however, fewer people were attending the events. Radio had become popular and people could hear speakers and entertainment in their homes. Finally the Chautauqua companies went out of business, but there are still reminders of that exciting week in many Iowa towns. The camping ground sometimes became a town park known as Chautauqua Park. People who attended Chautauqua can still recall the smell of the canvas tent and the thrill of the programs.

Even though many changes have taken place in education, some things are still the same. The Iowa school system still has both state and local levels, as it did in the nineteenth century.

People all over the nation recognize Iowa for its good system of public education. Some parents have chosen to educate their children at home, under the direction of their local schools. Young people who want to go to college have many choices. Iowa has fourteen community colleges, many fine private schools such as Cornell College, Drake University, and Grinnell College, and three state universities. At these schools, students can study hundreds of different subjects and may prepare for almost any profession. Good schools are very important for a state and are one of Iowa's greatest assets.

FURTHER READING

Bonney, Margaret, ed. "Going to School in Iowa." *The Goldfinch* 2, no. 4 (April 1981). Iowa City: State Historical Society of Iowa.

Cooper, Arnie. "A Stony Road: Black Education in Iowa, 1838–1860." *The Annals of Iowa* 48, nos. 3, 4 (Winter/Spring 1986). Iowa City: State Historical Society of Iowa.

1870 Iowa State Almanac. Explorations in Iowa History Project. Cedar Falls: Malcolm Price Laboratory School, University of Northern Iowa.

11 Keeping the Faith on the Frontier

*S*ettlers came to Iowa from other parts of America and from Europe, where they had been members of many different churches. Some belonged to no church at all. With such different religious beliefs and customs, there might have been tensions and struggles, but for the most part, disagreements were settled peacefully. Churches became an important part of Iowa life.

RELIGION IN AMERICA

When European settlers came to the New World, they brought with them their churches and ideas about God. In Europe, each country had a state (official) church. All citizens paid taxes to support the state church, regardless of their personal beliefs. Schools taught the beliefs of the state church as a regular part of education.

Because the New World attracted settlers from many countries with many different churches, no one religious group had enough members to become the state church for the whole nation. Members of each church objected to the idea of paying taxes to support other ministers, so the writers of the United States Constitution decided to have no state church. Instead, all churches are equal, and Americans are free to choose whichever one they wish or to choose no church at all. This is known as freedom of religion. The government will not interfere or favor one religion over another. This is called separation of church and state.

As a result, most communities have several different churches. While Americans are used to this situation today, it seemed very strange to early colonists. Some feared the system would never work because they thought that people with different beliefs could never live together peacefully. For example, even before Iowa became a state, there was a struggle involving the Latter Day Saints, sometimes known as Mormons.

THE MORMONS

The Mormon church was founded in New York in 1830 by Joseph Smith, who believed that God had called him to establish a holy city, Zion. The Mormons were driven from place to place until they settled in Nauvoo, Illinois, across the river from southeast Iowa. Nauvoo quickly grew into a city of 20,000 people. It had its own small army, the Nauvoo Legion, for protection and its own judges and courts.

Unfortunately, the Mormons had problems with their neighbors. The surrounding towns feared the growth of Nauvoo and disliked the Nauvoo Legion. They resented the Mormon claims that God would someday give them land to build Zion. There were rumors that Mormon men had several wives, a practice called polygamy, which most Americans strongly opposed. In 1844, Joseph Smith and his brother Hyrum were put in jail in

Carthage, a town about ten miles from Nauvoo. A mob attacked the jail and murdered the two Mormon leaders. Outnumbered and fearing more violence, the Mormons left Nauvoo.

In February 1846, the first Mormon wagons crossed the ice of the Mississippi River into Iowa, heading west through southern Iowa to a new land where they could worship as they pleased. The main body of Mormons followed in March. They were very well organized. The first groups made bridges, marked roads, dug wells for later wagons, and planted fields for the last groups to harvest. They established camps where weary travelers could rest and get supplies. Garden Grove in Decatur County and Mt. Pisgah in Union County were important stopping sites along the Mormon Trail.

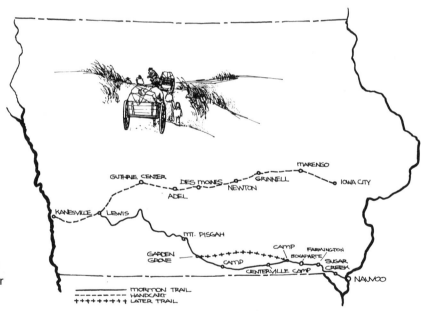

The Mormon routes across southern Iowa left roads for early settlers to follow.

When they reached the Missouri River, the Mormons made camp and built the town of Kanesville, which later became Council Bluffs. Across the river, they set up winter quarters. From there, they prepared to make the long trip across the Great Plains to the shores of the

164

Great Salt Lake in Utah. As many as 30,000 Mormons set out on the Mormon Trail. Many died from hunger and sickness, but thousands followed their leaders to their new home in the west. These persecuted people did much to open southern and western Iowa for settlement. Later pioneers used their bridges and wells and followed their well-marked trails.

Eight years after the first group reached the Salt Lake Valley (1855), another 1,300 Mormons passed through Iowa. They traveled between New York City and Iowa City by rail. From Iowa City to Salt Lake City they walked, pulling handcarts loaded with their few goods. To the Mormons in Liverpool, England, the Mormon leader Brigham Young wrote from America:

Mormon handcarts crossing Iowa on their way to Salt Lake City. Beginning in 1856, the handcart expedition to Utah started where the railroad stopped— in Iowa City.

Fifteen miles a day will bring them through in 70 days, and, after they get accustomed to it, they will travel 20, 25, or 30 with all ease, and no danger of giving out, but will continue to get stronger and stronger; the little ones and sick, if there are any, can be carried on the carts, but there will be none sick in a little time after they get started.

165

Archer Walters, a forty-seven-year-old carpenter from Sheffield, England, joined the handcart expedition at Iowa City. His wife, Harriet, and five children (Sarah, eighteen; Henry, sixteen; Harriet, fourteen; Martha, twelve; and Lydia, six) came with him. He stated that he would give his life if he could reach "the Valley of the Mountains in the Land of Zion, with my family, that they may grow up under the influence of the Gospel of Christ."

The Journal of Archer Walters from Iowa City to the Missouri River, 1856

June 11.   Journeyed 7 miles. Very dusty. All tired and smothered with dust and camped in the dust or where the dust blowed. Was captain over my tent of 18 in number but they were a family of Welsh and our spirits were not united. Had a tent but Bro. Ellsworth would not let me use it and had to leave my tent poles behind.

June 12.   Journeyed 12 miles. Went very fast with our handcarts. Harriet still very ill. . . .

June 15.   Got up about 4 o'clock to make a coffin for my brother John Lee's son named William Lee, aged 12 years. Meetings Sunday as usual and at the same time had to make another coffin for Sister Prator's child. Was tired with repairing handcarts the last week. Went and buried them by moonlight at Bear Creek.

June 16.   Harriet very ill. Traveled 19 miles and after pitching tent mended carts.

June 17.   Traveled about 17 miles; pitched tent. Made a little coffin for Bro. Job Welling's son and mended a handcart wheel. . . .

June 21.   Traveled about 13 miles. Camped at Indian Creek. Bro. Bowers died about 6 o'clock; from Birmingham Conference. Went to buy some wood to make the coffin but the kind farmer gave me the wood and nails. It had been a very hot day and I was never more tired, but God has said as my day my strength shall be.

June 26. Traveled about 1 mile. Very faint from lack of food. We are only allowed about ¾ lb. of flour a head each day and about 3 oz. of sugar each week. About ½ of a lb. of bacon each a week; which makes those that have no money very weak. Made a child's coffin for Sister Sheen—Emma Sheen aged 2½ years.

June 27. Got up before sunrise. Cut a tombstone on wood and bury the child before starting from camp.

June 28. . . . Rose soon after 4 o'clock. Started with high wind. Short of water and I was never more tired. Rested a bit after we camped then came on a thunder storm, and rain, blowed our tent down. Split the canvas and wet our clothes and we had to lay on the wet clothes and ground. . . .

June 29. Rather stiff in joints when we rose. . . Busy all day. My wife and Sarah mending. Short of provisions. Children crying for their dinner.

June 30. Rose in good health, except Harriet, and started with our handcarts with but little breakfast . . . but never traveled 17 miles more easily. . . . Sleep very well after prayers in tent.

July 3. Ever to be remembered Bro. Card gave me ½ dollar for making his daughter's coffin. Start with my cart before the camp as others had done but was told not to and had to suffer for it. Went the wrong way; about 30 of the brothers and sisters, and went 10½ miles the wrong way. We put our three handcarts together and made beds with all the clothes we had and laid down about ½ past 10 o'clock. 11 o'clock

> **Got up before sunrise. Cut a tombstone on wood and bury the child before starting from camp.**
> —Archer Walters (Mormon Handcart Expedition, 1856)

167

	Brother Butler who had charge of the mule teams came with the mules and wagon to fetch us. Got to camp when they were getting up. Laid down about an hour and started with the camp.
July 5.	A deer or elk served out to camp. Brother Parker brings into camp his little boy (age 6) that had been lost (3 days). Great joy right through the camp. The mother's joy I can not describe. Expect we are going to rest. Washing, etc., today. Jordan Creek. Made a pair of sashes for the old farmer. Indian meal; no flour. Slept well.
July 6.	Made 2 doors for . . . 3 dollars and boarded with farmer.
July 7.	Harriet better. Lydia poorly. Traveled about 20 miles.
July 8.	Traveled a round about road about 20 miles. Crossed the river Missouri and camped at the city of Florence. Very tired; glad to rest. Slept well. Lydia better and Harriet. All in good spirits. . . .

The Walters family reached Salt Lake City and Archer's journal ends on September 14, 1856. Two weeks later he died from dysentery caused by eating cornmeal and molasses. His wife and five children survived.

Some Mormons, however, objected to certain teachings of their leaders, especially on polygamy. Believing that no man should have more than one wife, they formed their own church, the Reorganized Latter Day Saints. Joseph Smith's son, also named Joseph Smith, became their leader. Instead of traveling west with the main group, they established the town of Lamoni in southern Iowa and founded Graceland College in 1895. Those who bought land in southern and western Iowa became some of the earliest settlers in these areas.

THE CATHOLICS

While many of the Mormons passed through Iowa and did not settle here, other religious groups came and stayed. From the days of the earliest American settlement in Iowa, Dubuque has been an important city for Catholics. Miners from Ireland, who were Catholic, came to work in the lead mines near the city. To minister to these men, Father Samuel Mazzuchelli, an Italian priest, came to Dubuque. There he helped to build St. Raphael's church. Before he returned to Italy in 1843, Father Mazzuchelli built seven Catholic churches in the area. In 1837, with more Catholics moving to the region, the Catholic Church created the Iowa Diocese. A diocese is a region under the direction of a Catholic bishop.

BISHOP LORAS

Bishop Mathias Loras was the first Catholic bishop in Iowa. The son of wealthy French parents, Loras arrived in Dubuque in 1839 and set to work. He established schools and founded a college, which was later named Loras College in his honor. He helped Catholic settlers to find good land in northeast Iowa and sometimes even picked out spots for new towns. When he encouraged poor Catholic families in eastern cities to come to Iowa, however, some eastern Catholic bishops resented his efforts to "steal" their members.

While Loras was bishop, the Catholic Church in Iowa grew rapidly. In the 1840s and 1850s, many Catholic families from Ireland and Germany migrated to Iowa. When Loras arrived in 1839, there were only a few Catholics in Iowa. By 1860, there were 31,000.

The Catholic Church grew rapidly under their first bishop, the hard-working and able Mathias Loras. At first, Catholic families immigrated from Ireland and Germany. After the Civil War, Czech and French Catholics moved to the state. Thirty years later, Italians and eastern European Catholics began moving into southern Iowa to work in the coal mines.

The New Melleray Abbey brought something of old Europe to northeast Iowa.

Though these immigrants belonged to the same church, they often preferred to worship with those from their native country. Many spoke only a little English and wanted to be with those who spoke their native languages and followed traditional customs. Therefore, in many cities several Catholic churches were built. In Iowa City, for example, Irish Catholics worshiped in one church, German Catholics in another, Czech Catholics in another, and English Catholics in still another.

THE CONGREGATIONALISTS

Unlike the Catholics, Congregationalists believed that each congregation should control its own affairs and not be under the direction of a bishop. Although the Congregational Church was not large in Iowa, its members often became important community leaders. Today it is called the United Church of Christ-Congregational.

Many Congregationalists were descended from the Puritans of New England. Because the church believed strongly in education, Congregational ministers studied religion in colleges and often spoke Latin and Greek. It took so much training to be a minister that the Congregationalists did not have as many as some other groups.

In New England, Congregationalists and members of other churches worried about the western areas of the United States, including Iowa. They feared that the settlers of the new lands would not have ministers, churches, or schools. To provide religion, they took the lead in organizing the American Home Mission Society, which raised money to send missionaries to the frontier states. On the frontier, Presbyterians and Congregationalists often worshiped together since their beliefs were similar. Sometimes they voted to become a single group.

In 1838, the first Congregational Church was established in the little town of Denmark in southeast Iowa. The Reverend Asa Turner first came west to preach and teach in Illinois with a group of ministers called the Illinois Band. As settlers began crossing into Iowa, Turner saw the need for his work in the new territory "across the river."

In 1843, a group of college students in Massachusetts decided to become missionaries to the western states. They wrote to Turner asking questions about the new land. What was the weather like? What clothes

Each to found a church, all to found a college.
—**Pledge of the Iowa Band (1844)**

171

should they bring? Was the new territory safe for women? Turner urged them to come to Iowa. Eleven students responded to his call and became known as the Iowa Band. They gathered in Turner's church in Denmark and chose towns where they would begin their work. They founded many churches and became leading citizens in their new homes. They also started a college in Davenport known as Iowa College. Several years later, the college moved to Grinnell and became Grinnell College.

The Congregational Church did not grow rapidly in the new state. The ministers often taught school through the week. This was a valuable service but left little time for seeking new members for their churches as other ministers did.

THE METHODISTS

The largest denomination on the Iowa frontier was the Methodist Church. Methodists built their first church in Dubuque in 1834. The Iowa legislature held its sessions in the Old Zion Methodist Church in Burlington for a few years because it was the best building in the city.

The Methodists used local readers to teach Bible classes and local people to lead worship services. Circuit riders (traveling ministers) visited each congregation in their areas as often as they could. When the group grew large enough, they had a full-time minister. In this way, the church could reach new areas and support new congregations. The Methodist Church grew rapidly on the frontier. By the Civil War, it was the largest church in Iowa, with 90,000 members.

Methodist circuit riders traveled on horseback to reach new settlers on the frontier.

A STATE OF MANY FAITHS

There were many other religious groups in the state. Settlers from northern Europe were often Lutherans, the third largest church in Iowa. The Lutheran church was often the center of Scandinavian immigrant communities. Dutch settlers were members of the Reformed Church. Mennonite and Amish groups came to the New World from Germany and finally settled in Iowa. Quakers started many communities in Iowa during the 1800s, including West Branch and New Providence. Some Quaker groups had left the South because they did not like slavery. Baptists also came to the Iowa frontier. In the 1800s, Baptist ministers were called preacher-farmers because they farmed during the week and preached on Sunday.

A small number of Jews settled in Iowa in the mid-1800s. They built places of worship called synagogues in

173

several Iowa frontier towns and took an active part in community affairs. The earliest Jewish settlers in Iowa were immigrants from Germany, but later Jewish immigrants arrived from Russia and other countries in eastern Europe.

In recent years, Southeast Asian families settling in Iowa, particularly in Des Moines, have brought Buddhism to Iowa's prairies. The Islamic community in Cedar Rapids takes pride in being the first in the nation to build its own mosque.

There have always been Iowans who are members of no religious organization. As early as the Civil War era, only one-third of the population were members of any church.

IMPORTANCE OF EARLY CHURCHES

Often, a church was one of the few organizations in a frontier community. Church meetings were important in bringing settlers together. They met for church picnics, potluck suppers, and other activities. Early schools often met in church buildings through the week.

Many churches had strict rules that they expected their members to follow. There were rules against swearing and drinking alcohol. Some rules ordered debts to be paid promptly and cheerfully. Others demanded that members ask forgiveness from those they had upset. Since there were few law officers on the frontier, churches played an important role in getting people to live together peacefully.

Men and women from different Protestant churches often joined together in clubs called lodges. The Masonic lodge was one of the largest lodges for men, and the

> Our church [Methodist] frowned on drinking, smoking, dancing, the theater, and card playing.
> —Bruce Bliven ("A Prairie Boyhood," Emmetsburg, around 1900)

174

Settlers could meet at church social functions like this one at the Methodist church in Solon.

Eastern Star was an important women's organization. Though the lodges were not churches, they included worship activities in their meetings. Members prayed, read the Bible, and encouraged each other to lead good lives. Most lodges also had secret ceremonies known only to their members. Meeting once or twice a month, often in their own lodge halls, members wore special costumes and called their officers by grand titles like "Exalted Master."

Many of Iowa's early colleges were founded by religious organizations. Churches were anxious to train ministers, and early colleges often taught courses in religion. The Methodists were associated with several colleges, including Iowa Wesleyan, Cornell College, Simpson, Upper Iowa, and Morningside. The Presbyterians founded the University of Dubuque, Coe College, and Buena Vista. Wartburg College and Luther College were Lutheran schools. The Baptists founded Central University in Pella, but the Dutch Reformed Church took it over and renamed it Central College. The Dutch also established Dordt College and Northwestern College in northwest Iowa. The Disciples of Christ established Drake University in Des Moines. The Quakers founded William Penn College in Oskaloosa. The Catholics established six colleges around the state: Clarke, Loras, Marycrest, St. Ambrose, Briar Cliff, and Mt. Mercy.

These private colleges have played an important part in the history of education, providing opportunities for higher education for many Iowans. Many colleges are now independent of the churches that established them. Churches, however, still take an active interest in education.

SOCIAL ISSUES

Most churches believe that they have a duty to improve society and want to put this belief into practice. The problem is that not everyone agrees on what makes an improvement. Churches even disagree among themselves. Nevertheless, several important issues in Iowa have involved religious opinions.

Slavery

Before the Civil War, the Quakers and Congregationalists took the lead in demanding an end to slavery. Even though it was against the law, they helped runaway slaves escape to freedom. These churches supported political candidates who promised to try to pass laws against slavery.

Sabbath Laws

Some churches, including the Methodists, Congregationalists, Presbyterians, and Baptists, once favored limiting what could be done on Sunday. They believed that Sunday should be a day of rest and worship only. Pushed by the churches, the Iowa legislature passed laws forbidding stores to open on Sunday. Sunday baseball games and other amusements were made illegal. These were often called "Blue Laws." However, many groups from Europe wanted the social activities and recreation that they had been used to on Sunday afternoon in their home countries. After a while, support for the restrictions faded, and the laws were changed.

BASEBALLS, BIBLES, AND BILLY SUNDAY

One of America's most famous preachers was once a baseball player. Billy Sunday was born in Ames in 1862 during the Civil War. His father, a soldier in the Union Army, died before the war was over. Billy and his older brother were first sent to homes for orphans in Glenwood and Davenport and then to their grandfather's farm near Nevada.

When Billy was going to Nevada High School, he earned a great reputation as a speedy baseball player. He could run around the bases in record time. In 1883, the manager of a Chicago team watched him play in Marshalltown and signed him up as a professional player then and there. For the next eight years, Billy played baseball in Chicago.

In 1887, Billy Sunday was drinking beer with some friends in a saloon in Chicago. When he left, a religious revival meeting was going on across the street. When he heard those "gospel hymns I used to hear my mother sing back in the log cabin in Iowa," Billy sat down on the curb and began to cry. He did not like the way he was living.

That afternoon changed his life. He vowed to live

State Historical Society

177

from then on as he thought God wanted him to live. He became an active member of a Presbyterian church in Chicago. Although he continued to play baseball, he would not play games on Sunday because he considered it wrong to play sports on the Sabbath. Finally, he gave up his $500 a month baseball salary and went to work for the Young Men's Christian Association (YMCA). His new job paid only $83 a month.

In 1896 Billy Sunday began a series of preaching meetings. Very quickly, he was as much of a success as he had been on the baseball field. He became famous for his preaching style. Sunday told jokes and talked about his baseball career. He spoke out strongly against drinking alcohol. When he became excited, he would leap around the platform, pound the pulpit, or even throw a chair. He urged listeners to give their lives to Christ.

Large crowds came to hear him. In Philadelphia and New York, he preached to thousands of people at a time. In his lifetime, he may have preached to one hundred million people. Some say Billy Sunday converted seven hundred thousand men and women to the Christian faith.

He died in 1933 when he was seventy-one years old.

Sunday had given orders on what his funeral should be. "No sad stuff when I go. No black, no crepe, no tears." Instead, those at his funeral sang Billy's favorite "Glory Song."

> Oh, that will be glory for me,
> Glory for me, glory for me,
> When by His Grace I shall look on His face,
> That will be glory for me.

Gambling

Many churches objected to dancing and gambling. Sometimes communities forbade dance halls. For a long time, the state made gambling illegal. But in more recent years, a law was passed to make the game of bingo, a form of gambling, legal in Iowa. Players pay money to play, and winners get a prize. Any money left after prizes are awarded must go to churches or charity. In 1985, Iowa created a public lottery, another form of gambling. Profits from the lottery support public projects. Dog and horse racing and riverboat gambling have recently become legal pastimes in Iowa.

Prohibition

For many years, the most important issue involving churches was the sale of alcohol. Many churches considered drinking alcohol to be evil. Pointing to many problems that alcohol abuse causes, some people wanted to prohibit (forbid) making or selling liquor. They were called prohibitionists. For a time, they were successful. In 1919, the whole nation came under a law forbidding anyone to make or sell alcohol. National prohibition lasted for sixteen years.

Private Schools

The state requires all children to attend schools that meet certain standards. Some church groups have wanted to educate their children in their own schools so that religion could be included in the curriculum. When the church schools did not meet state standards, the churches usually had to stop their private classes. Today about 10 percent of Iowa's children are educated in church schools or church-related schools approved by the state.

Other Social Issues

In recent years, the churches have been active on many issues. They have raised money to feed hungry people in this country and around the world. Many churches helped to find homes for refugees from wars in Southeast Asia and Latin America. Churches have also worked to promote peace.

There continues to be disagreement on some important topics, such as whether there should be prayer in public schools and how the earth was created. As long as people are free to worship as they want, there will be differences of opinion on many issues.

Religious groups have played an important part in educating and shaping Iowa communities. Churches were some of the first organizations on the frontier. Because there have been so many different religious groups in the state, Iowans have had to learn to tolerate people with beliefs different from their own.

FURTHER READING

Launius, Roger D. "The Mormon Quest for a Perfect Society at Lamoni, Iowa, 1870–1890." *The Annals of Iowa* 47, no. 4 (Spring 1984). Iowa City: State Historical Society of Iowa.

Journal of Archer Walters. Explorations in Iowa History Project. Cedar Falls: Malcolm Price Laboratory School, University of Northern Iowa.

12 Experiments in Community Living

During the 1800s most people came to Iowa with only their own families, but some came as part of a larger group. These people were called communitarians, from the word community. Members of communitarian groups shared beliefs about how they should live and what they should believe. They settled close together. In fact, members of some groups owned property together. Most communitarians believed that they should separate themselves from outsiders if they were to remain true to their beliefs. The groups that settled in Iowa were the Icarians, the Society of True Inspiration (the Amana Colonies), and the Old Order Amish. The Icarians disbanded in the 1890s, but the Inspirationalists and Amish still live in Iowa today.

THE ICARIANS

The Icarians began in France in the 1840s because of a book. Etienne Cabet, a French lawyer and politician, wrote *Voyage to Icaria,* in which he described a make-believe country where everyone lived happily. In this country, called Icaria, everyone was equal and everyone had the same amount of money. Everyone did the same amount of work. Instead of individuals owning property, the people together owned all the property. (This is called socialism.) Some people in France who read *Voyage to Icaria* wanted to start such a society.

Fearful that they would not be allowed to build a community like Icaria in France, the group traveled to the United States. A few French people arrived in Texas, but they did not like the climate. They heard about Nauvoo, Illinois, where Mormons leaving for Utah were anxious to sell or rent their buildings. The Icarians decided to move there. Finally, the Icarians bought land in Adams County, Iowa. In 1855, they left Nauvoo and moved to their 3,000 acres near the town of Corning in southwest Iowa. By this time the Icarian membership had fallen to 239 people.

Unlike Nauvoo, the land in Iowa had never been farmed. That meant the Icarians had to work much harder, breaking the sod for the first time and building new homes. It took great effort to create their home in Iowa. After a few years though, the Icarians had developed a comfortable place to live. They built small log cabins for each family and larger buildings for dining, laundry, sewing, and other activities. Together, members planted crops, raised gardens, and started raising cattle and sheep.

In Iowa, the Icarians continued their socialistic way of life. Instead of each family owning a farm, the Icarians as a group owned all land and property. Each person owned only his or her own clothes and a few personal items. To manage their operation, they elected officers.

The Icarians believed that all members should share activities and take turns doing different tasks. Instead of having kitchens in the houses, all the members came to the community dining hall to eat their meals.

Icarian children were raised in a special way. Around age two, all children went to the nursery where they were cared for by older women. Toys were shared and each child was expected to think of the feelings of others. With their children at the nursery, the mothers went to work in the kitchen, laundry, garden, or sewing room.

Sketch map of the Icarian settlement in the 1870s.

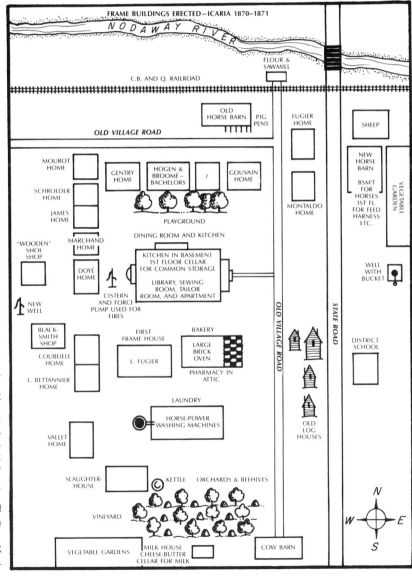

The Icarians believed that education was important. Many older members who had come from France taught French and several other languages in the Corning area. Every year the group put on musical concerts and operettas. Members also presented lectures on scientific topics. They had a large library and encouraged their members to read constantly.

After the Icarians had lived in Adams County for about ten years, the older members were pleased with their lives. The younger people, however, believed that their parents had forgotten their earlier fine ideas. They wanted the Icarians to expand by bringing in new members and starting new businesses. The older members wanted to leave things as they were.

Because of these disagreements, the younger Icarians decided to split away from the main group. In 1870, the older and younger members divided up the land and property. The older ones then moved to a new site a few miles away. This made two communities, New Icaria and Old Icaria.

After the split the younger members did not do well. Within a few years they decided to leave Iowa for California, but even there they did not stay together for very long.

A gathering of the last Icarians at their colony in Adams County, around 1880.

State Historical Society

The older Icarians stayed near Corning until 1895. By then, their membership had dwindled to twenty-five and they did not have enough people to do the farm work. With great sadness, the group voted to disband. They divided the land and money among all their members. People who had been with the Icarians the longest received the most land and money.

After Icaria's breakup, some members returned to France. Others stayed near Corning and continued to farm, only this time as individual property owners. Some members headed south because they wanted a warmer climate.

Several Icarians wrote about their lives at Corning. One of these was Maria Marchand Ross, who wrote *Child of Icaria*. Even though there was much fighting among the adult Icarians, for example, over who had to work harder, Mrs. Ross remembered a secure, happy childhood.

The Icarians broke up mostly because the older and younger members simply could not agree on the group's goals. All agreed, however, that such things as everybody doing the same amount of work and everyone living in the same type of home were good ideas. For several generations, the Icarians succeeded in building what they thought was a better society. By 1895, however, it had come to an end.

> **Women take part in the deliberations of the assembly . . . they can offer their opinion and counsel, but are not permitted to vote.**
> **—William Hinds (Icaria, 1878)**

THE SOCIETY OF TRUE INSPIRATION

While the Icarians were settling in western Iowa, other communitarians were settling in eastern Iowa. In 1855, the Society of True Inspiration came to Iowa County and built six villages—South Amana, East

Amana, West Amana, High Amana, Middle Amana, and Main Amana. They chose the name Amana because it means "remain faithful." A short time later, they bought additional land, including the village of Homestead. In total, the Inspirationalists bought about twenty-six thousand acres of land and owned seven villages.

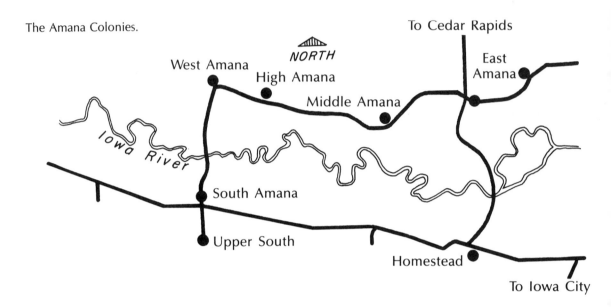

The Amana Colonies.

The Inspirationalists started in Germany in the early 1700s, when they left the Lutheran Church because they wanted a simpler religion. The name comes from their religious practices. Some members who believed they received inspirations or messages from God were called *Werkzeuges,* which meant tools of God. The *Werkzeuges* wrote down the messages, and these became the group's religious beliefs.

In Germany, the Inspirationalists were treated badly, and they were not allowed to buy land. So the group decided to come to America for land and for freedom. Christian Metz was their *Werkzeug* and leader in the plans to immigrate.

186

Once in America, the Inspirationalists settled near Ebenezer, New York. In the 1850s, they came to Iowa because it was not crowded and the group felt that they must separate themselves from outsiders. Here they found good farmland for sale that included some timber stands and had a river flowing through it. With the land, trees, and water supply, the Inspirationalists could set up factories and also raise crops and animals.

The Inspirationalists lived a simple life. All members dressed in plain, dark clothing. Families did not own their own houses but lived in homes provided by church leaders. Amana homes did not have kitchens because it saved time to prepare food in a few large kitchens. Also, the Inspirationalists believed that members who came together to eat could talk together and would feel closer to one another. Each village had several kitchens and each kitchen served about forty people. The women prepared and cooked the food under a kitchen boss.

Every adult person in Amana had to work. The church elders picked some people to be supervisors, but most members moved from job to job. Men worked in

A street in the Amana Colonies around 1936.

187

the fields, cared for animals, and labored in the factories. Women worked in the kitchens, tended the gardens, and did the laundry. Older women cared for the children. In the Amana villages, no one job was to be any more important than any other.

Amana women making sauerkraut at Homestead in the 1920s.

State Historical Society

The Amana people believed in living their religion through their daily lives. They thought it was selfish of people to think only of themselves. Instead, everyone was to think of ways to please God and help one another. Each village had a church and each church had several elders. The elders were older men whom everyone respected. They handled all religious matters and also handled the community's day-to-day affairs. If someone broke a rule, the elders saw that the person was punished. Although the colonies had no jails, guilty persons were punished in other ways. For example, the wrong-doer had to sit in the front bench in church for everyone to see. The Inspirationalists went to church eleven times a week. There they listened to the elders preach and were reminded of the proper way to live. Once a year, each member confessed his or her sins in church.

The Amana communities did well in Iowa. They had selected good land for farming and they worked hard to operate their factories, which also sold furniture and cloth to outsiders. After a while, however, they began to feel that they should not have to work so hard. To help with the work, especially the unpleasant work, outsiders were hired. Soon, over two hundred outsiders were working in the seven Amana colonies.

State Historical Society

Amana carpenter making a wagon wheel.

By the 1880s, the last two *Werkzeuges,* Christian Metz and Barbara Heinemann, had died, and the Amanas began to have serious trouble. The people did not listen to the elders as well as they had listened to the *Werkzeuges.* More and more Inspirationalists began to

189

drink alcohol and to miss church. Parents bought toys for their children that the elders had forbidden, such as bicycles. People began to play cards and hold parties to celebrate birthdays and Christmas. The elders taught that these practices were wrong, but many people did them anyway.

A CHILDHOOD IN AMANA

An Amana childhood was somewhat different from that of other children. Young people in Amana had many rules to follow. There were some toys that they could not play with and they had to wear simple, dark clothing. However, surrounded by many family members, Amana children felt secure and loved. They saw relatives daily and often stayed with grandparents or aunts and uncles.

Most mothers worked in the Amana Colonies, so at age two, children started going to the village nursery during the day. All Amana children went to school when they reached age five or six. The school day was divided into three parts. First, the children learned basic subjects like reading. Next, they had time to play. And finally, students learned to do things with their hands, such as knitting for the girls and woodwork for the boys. Sometimes children did farm work like helping with the harvest. In the Amanas, children went to school in summer as well as in winter.

When they reached age fourteen, Amana children finished school and were given jobs. Many stayed with the same type of work for the rest of their lives. Sometimes they liked their work and sometimes they did not. Girls went to work in the kitchens, gardens, or laundry. Some boys went to work in the factories while others learned to do farm work. The village elders made the decisions about where each young person would work.

190

They knew each child well and they had a good idea of what work each child could do.

The elders believed that children should be quiet most of the time. In fact, they had "Sixty-six Rules for the Conduct of Children." One rule was that children should "walk quietly and mannerly" when they were going to and from school. Another rule said that at mealtime, children should be quiet unless they were asked a question.

Only a few Amana children (always boys) went to high school and college. The Inspirationalists believed that the villages should have their own professional people such as physicians, lawyers, and veterinarians. Since these people had to have professional training, the elders selected certain boys to go on to high school and college. The young men usually went to high school in nearby Marengo and then to the University of Iowa or Iowa State University.

Through their upbringing, Amana children learned to work hard and to adapt themselves to their communal lifestyle. In many ways, the schooling of the Amana children before 1932 was much like that of the Amish children today.

As members paid less attention to their leaders, they grew more interested in the outside world. A railroad ran through the village of Homestead bringing visitors to the colonies. The Inspirationalists were spending more time with outsiders and were less interested in their own special way of life.

After World War I, the communities faced financial trouble. In 1923, two big fires burned down a large flour mill and a gristmill. Also, the Amana people made less money during the 1920s because outsiders had less money to spend on products from the villages. These problems grew worse in the early 1930s when the entire country went into a bad economic slump, or depression. Amana leaders could see only two choices. First, they could go on with their communal life, but they would have to let the two hundred outside workers go and the members would have to work harder themselves. Or second, they could give up their communal way of life and live more like other Iowans.

In 1932, the Inspirationalists voted on the issue. When the votes were counted it was clear the Amana people had voted for a change. Only the older people in the villages wanted to keep the old ways. All they knew was a communal life and they were afraid that if things changed, no one would take care of them.

After the vote, the Inspirationalists picked a group of men to handle the business matters. These men made up the Amana Society and took care of the land and factories. People in the Amanas continued to work, but they were paid for what they did. Today, the Amana Society still handles all the business of the Amana colonies.

The older people did not need to worry. Everyone was given stock in the Amana properties, there was no fight over community property, and everyone was able to live well. Amana people still get help from the Amana

Society, including medical, dental, and burial insurance.

Today many people in the Amana villages are relatives or descendants of the first Inspirationalists. They work there or in nearby communities, and many still attend the Amana Church. In many ways, they live like people outside the colonies, but they still think of themselves as belonging to a special group. They think of themselves as Inspirationalists and take great pride in their history.

THE OLD ORDER AMISH

The third communitarian society in Iowa is the Old Order Amish. This group settled in Iowa in the 1840s. Because they refuse to drive automobiles they are sometimes called the "horse and buggy people." They are also called "plain people" because they dress in a simple manner. Today there are Old Order Amish near Kalona, Oelwein, Milton, Bloomfield, Riceville, and McIntire. Altogether there are about two thousand Old Order Amish in Iowa.

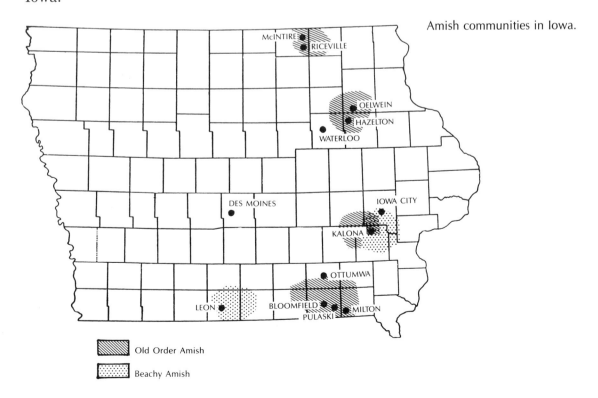

Amish communities in Iowa.

In the 1690s, a Mennonite minister in Switzerland, Jacob Ammann, started the Amish group. The Amish remained in Europe for about one hundred years but then began immigrating to the United States. The first immigrants settled in Pennsylvania, but after that, Amish families found other places. They arrived in Iowa in the late 1840s. The Amish had been farmers in the eastern states and they wanted to continue that work in Iowa. They first settled in Johnson and Washington counties in eastern Iowa.

Until the 1850s, they were all simply known as Amish. But then a new group was started, who called themselves the Old Order Amish. These Amish had split off from the others because they did not want to adopt new inventions and new clothing styles. They believed that God wanted them to live as they always lived in the past. The Old Order Amish also believed that God wanted them to hold services in their homes rather than in a separate church. They thought all members should wear the same type of clothing so people could immediately tell that they were Amish. They believed deeply that all Amish people should live on farms rather than in towns and cities.

Two Old Order Amish discuss local affairs at Kalona.

State Historical Society

In the 1920s another group, the Beachy Amish, split off from the Old Order because they wanted to have automobiles and telephones. In many ways the Beachy have the same religious views as the Old Order but live in a more modern way. Beachy Amish families may have automobiles, but they must be black. Their homes are electrified and they have separate church buildings for worship. In Iowa, about one-fifth of the Amish are Beachy, and they live near Kalona and Leon.

Today the Old Order Amish still live on farms and each Amish family owns its own land. This means that they do not live communally. An Amish farm has around one hundred acres where they raise corn, barley, oats, and hay. They also raise many hogs. Most Amish farmers use horses for their farming, although in Kalona they can use tractors. The Amish do not use commercial fertilizers, herbicides, or insecticides. Instead they use manure for fertilizer and pull the weeds. In fact, they farm in the way that many Iowans farmed in the 1920s.

Amish farmers threshing their grain on a farm near Kalona. The Amish have threshing rings where several families come together to do the work.

Joan Liffring-Zug

195

The Old Order Amish have large families, with as many as eight or ten children. Even when the children are quite young, girls help their mothers care for the younger children and assist with housework and Amish boys help their fathers with outside farm work.

The Amish have strong religious beliefs. One of the beliefs is adult baptism, which means that Amish boys and girls are not baptized until around age fifteen. The Amish also believe that they will remain Amish, and follow all the Amish practices, only if they do not mix with outsiders. They call this idea separation from the world. Finally, the Amish are peaceful people who do not believe in war. Because their consciences made them object to war, they are called conscientious objectors.

For the close-knit Amish families, Sunday is the most important day of the week. They hold church services in members' homes every other Sunday. The family who is hosting church must clean the house from top to bottom to get ready. Families arrive for church around 9 A.M. The father unhitches the horses, and if it is cold, he puts them in the barn. In nice weather, the men stand around and visit in the barnyard. The women usually head for the house, along with the smaller children. Around 9:30, the service begins with several hymns, which the Amish sing slowly and without any musical instruments.

The Amish have both a bishop and several ministers. First a minister presents a short sermon for about thirty minutes. Then the bishop presents the long sermon that lasts about one and one-half hours. After church, the host family serves a large lunch. Most people remain through the afternoon, visiting and catching up on neighborhood activities. Then, around 4 P.M., it is time to start for home so the men can do the chores.

196

The Amish expect to help each other. If an Amish person gets sick, the neighbors help pay the doctor's bill. If an Amishman is injured and cannot do his farm work, then Amish neighbors help out. If an Amish family loses a barn or house through fire, other Amish people give both money and labor to rebuild it.

Amish people in Iowa also help Amish families in other states. Most of them read an Amish newspaper, *The Budget,* that is published in Sugarcreek, Ohio. This newspaper carries news about Amish communities not only in the United States but also in Canada and Central America. If an Amish family in Iowa has trouble, Amish families in many different places send money to the Iowa family. This is a major way that the plain people help one another.

Old Order Amish building a barn near Kalona, 1970s. Amish farmers still have barn raisings where the neighbors all come to help out. Sometimes the Amish call this a frolic.

Joan Liffring-Zug

Two columns from the Amish Mennonite newspaper, *The Budget,* published in Sugarcreek, Ohio, 1984.

KEOTA, IOWA

Salem Mennonite Fellowship

Apr. 17--A sunny pleasant morning.

Tues. supper guests of John Mark Millers were the Philip Martin family of Boyd, Wisc. They spent the night at Walter Beachys'.

Fri. p.m.: a number of sisters met at the church kitchen to make an abundant supply of noodles for our Belize mission workers.

Jesse Millers attended the funeral on Sun. of a stepbrother, Jacob J. Miller at Plain City, Ohio. Jesse's sisters, Viola Gingerich and Anna Mae Beachy, went along.

Visitors in church Sun. (morning and evening) were Paul Hostetlers and dau. of Mt. View, Ark. They were here visiting in his parents' home, the Emmet Hostetlers'.

Council meeting was held Sun. morning in preparation for communion service in two weeks.

Wilford Stutzman drove his pickup pulling a small house trailer down to Seymour, Mo. are Mon. They are planning to put a camper on the pickup, and is to be driven to Belize by the Edwin Miller family of Summersville, Mo. The Millers expect to replace the David Stutzmans while they are home on furlough, starting in May. Davids plan to come home via the camper; the house trailer is to be used by the James Yoders as a supplement to their native house.

Martha Stoddard is having a checkup with her doctor in Iowa City today.

Rachel Stutzman has been helping out in the Stoddard home, preparing meals and being with Martha so Glen can be out. She can go home at night. Mary E. Bender's back problem flared up so she is not at the Stoddards' at present.

Mrs. Alton Miller

KALONA, IOWA

April 16--The weather remains cool, cloudy and damp.

Anna Laura, the 8-year-old daughter of Edward and Ida (Miller) Schlabach, had an operation for appendicitis, on Saturday.

Yesterday, Willis, son of Daniel C. Masts of Coalgate, Okla. and Gloria, daughter of Pre. Mark A. Millers, were published for marriage. The wedding is to be May 10th. Willis has been living with us for over 2 years already, so he is about like our son. He is farming our place this year, so I guess we will also get a daughter!

Mrs. John N. Borntrager and children of Anabel, Mo. were here last week to visit her parents, John S. Yoder Jrs.

Saturday was the sale of the household goods of Miss Lena M. Yoder, at the property in Kalona. Lena is with her niece, Mrs. Edna Yoder, for several years already, and no one was in her house. She sold the house recently, and Lydia May Yoder will move into it before long. Lena had some old fashioned things which brought fancy prices. The glass cupboard brought over $500; a small earthen pot around $70, a small kerosene lamp, $80, nice china dishes, around $18 each. A 4 piece set of creamer, sugar bowl, spoon holder and butter dish went for $125.

Andy Helmuths and Irvin Gingerichs returned home Wednesday from their winter's stay in Florida. John R. Knepps returned home from Florida last week.

Mrs. Tobe Detweiler, Mrs. Amos Mast and daughter Salina and Mrs. Levi Yoder of Jamesport, Mo. were visitors in this community last week. Mrs. Yoder visited her aged mother, Mrs. Barbara Chupp and the others had come to visit Mrs. John S. Yoder Jr.

M. E. G.

Amish religious beliefs affect their views toward education. They believe strongly that eight years of schooling are enough for their children. After that, Amish parents teach their children at home. In some ways, the home education is like vocational education. Amish fathers teach their sons how to farm and care for livestock and Amish mothers teach their daughters how to cook, sew, and care for children. Amish parents are fearful that if their children go to high school or college, they will not want to remain Amish.

Amish children enjoy school and study hard. As well as learning how to read, write, and work arithmetic problems, they are taught to respect adults. All Amish children obey their teachers. One Old Order Amishman said the Amish children are taught the 4 R's – reading, 'riting, 'rithmetic, *and* respect. Amish children study most of the courses that non-Amish children study. One difference though is that they do not have music or physical education. Amish parents do not think that music is important and they believe that their children get enough exercise walking to school and doing chores at home.

> **In our schools we teach the four R's rather than the three R's: reading, 'riting, 'rithmetic, *and* respect.**
> **—Old Order Amishman (Kalona, 1971)**

An Old Order Amish buggy travels along a country road near Kalona. The Old Order do not believe in using modern vehicles.

Joan Liffring-Zug

Every year, the number of Old Order Amish in Iowa grows just a bit larger. In the past fifteen years, they have started a new community near the towns of Riceville and McIntire. Because of their large families and their belief that everyone should live on a farm, the Amish often buy land. When a young couple marries, the parents usually help them get a farm of their own.

Because of this steady need for more land, the Amish may face problems in Iowa. Farmland is expensive, sometimes too expensive for them to buy. At other times there is not enough land for sale. Eventually the Amish may find it impossible to buy more land here at reasonable prices. But at least for now, the Amish feel that Iowa is a good place to live.

During the past one hundred and forty years, Iowa has been home to many different groups of people. Some—the Icarians and the Inspirationalists—were communitarians who believed in a communal life. When they faced problems, however, the Icarians lost members and disbanded. The Inspirationalists solved their problems by changing their way of life. The Old Order Amish have been the most successful communitarians in Iowa. Instead of living a communal life, however, they share many activities and beliefs.

Iowa's communitarian societies remind us that people with different lifestyles have lived together in our state. A good state is one where different groups can live side by side and respect each other's views.

FURTHER READING

Andelson, Jonathan G. "Tradition, Innovation, and Assimilation in Iowa's Amana Colonies." *The Palimpsest* 69, no. 1 (Spring 1988). Iowa City: State Historical Society of Iowa.

Schwieder, Elmer, and Dorothy Schwieder. *A Peculiar People: Iowa's Old Order Amish.* Ames: Iowa State University Press, 1975.

Smith, Martha Browning. "The Story of Icaria." In *Patterns and Perspectives in Iowa History,* Dorothy Schwieder, ed. Ames: Iowa State University Press, 1973.

Yambura, Barbara. *A Change and a Parting.* Ames: Iowa State University Press, 1960.

13 Life on the Farm—Iowa Style

Agriculture has always been important in Iowa, which is known throughout the nation as a major farm state. During the nineteenth century, most Iowans lived on farms. Farming is still Iowa's most important industry, although most Iowans now live in cities and towns. Today, living on a farm is not too different from living in town, but for many years farm living and town living were very different.

LATE-NINETEENTH-CENTURY FARM LIFE

After the Civil War, Iowa was no longer a pioneer state. By 1865, there were farms and towns in every one of Iowa's ninety-nine counties. The farmers soon realized that they had settled on rich land and that many different crops would grow in Iowa. They usually raised one main crop each year even though that crop might change from time to time.

During the Civil War, Iowa farmers raised wheat for flour and made a good profit. After the war, however, they could not compete with new settlers in the Dakotas,

Kansas, and Nebraska, who were also raising wheat. So in Iowa, farmers turned to other crops. They quickly found that Iowa's climate and soil were just right for raising corn.

Iowa farmers learned something else about raising corn. Once they had harvested the crop, they had two choices—either sell the corn or feed it to pigs. Most farmers made more money feeding the corn to pigs and then selling the pigs. And so in the 1870s, Iowa's main farm products became corn and hogs.

For many years, Iowa farmers made the most money on hogs. We know this because farm families kept good business records. William and John Savage were farmers who settled in Henry County shortly before the Civil War. The two men, father and son, kept complete records that show their sales and profits. In 1880, the Savages made $767.12 on the sale of hogs. They also sold other items, including wool, grain, a few cows, and apples. One year they made $161 on apples.

Like other Iowa farmers, the Savages also raised barley, oats, and hay to feed to their animals. Raising many different crops (called diversified farming) was a safer way to farm. If one crop failed, the farmer still had others to use or sell.

TURN-OF-THE-CENTURY FARM LIFE

Horses were the most important animals on Iowa farms in 1900. They provided the pulling power for the farm implements, such as plows, corn planters, and hay rakes. They also pulled the buggies and wagons that carried farm families to town. Horses were used in teams of two, which were often about the same size. Although

202

farmers needed to work their horses hard, they usually treated them well and gave them pet names like Pete and Molly.

On the farm, family members still did their work according to the seasons. In the spring, farmers plowed their fields. In the summer, they cultivated (broke up) the soil to kill weeds. If they raised sheep, farmers sheared the animals in late spring. Throughout the summer, they cut the hay, which provided feed for horses and cows. Later, they harvested the wheat, barley, and oats. In the fall, after the corn was picked, farmers repaired fences and farm buildings. They also fattened the hogs for sale in November or December.

Hand-picking corn was still the hardest job. It started in October, and might take the whole family several cold months to finish. Once the harvest was safely in the corncrib, everyone felt better.

State Historical Society

A farmer picking corn by hand and throwing the ears into the wagon.

During the winter season (when the meat would not spoil), farm families usually butchered a hog and a cow, which provided meat for about six months. The meat was fixed in several different ways. Women canned most of it, but sometimes they smoked the pork to make hams. Even the pigs' intestines were used for sausage casings. In fact, farm women often said that they used all of the pig except the squeal!

Like their husbands, farm women also did their work by the seasons. During the winter, they made most of the family clothing and caught up on their mending. Farm families were often large, so women had a great deal of mending to do.

CHICKEN CHORES

Raising chickens took a lot of time. Each spring it was necessary to clean out the chicken coops and make up fresh nests. Lizzie Fellows Heckart, who lived in Van Buren County, remembers:

By the time I was nine or ten the setting of hens and caring for them and the little chickens was my job. We had a woodshed we used for the setting hens. First I would clean the shed wall, then spray with lime, and place the nests around the room with boards to cover them till the hens were sure they wanted to raise families.

When the time came, the nests were dusted with lime, fresh soft straw was put in them, and the hens were sprinkled with powder to discourage any insects. Fifteen eggs were carefully placed in a nest. Then after dark I would take Mrs. Hen gently up from where she wanted to set, tuck her head under my arm to keep her in the dark so she would not be frightened, and transfer her to her home for a three weeks' stay.

After the chicks hatched, they had to be watched that they did not crowd into one corner and suffocate. If

For farm women, the spring season involved the greatest amount of work. First, they had to make soap. All winter long they had collected animal fat and ashes to make lye. With these two ingredients, they made soap by boiling the lye and fat together until it thickened into soap. Then came a complete housecleaning. Many farm homes had coal-burning stoves, which left a layer of soot and ashes throughout the house. Spring-cleaning was an important custom in towns and cities as well. House-wives cleaned everything. Carpets were carried outside

it rained, they had so little sense that they might drown. Farm wives collected the eggs daily and also fed the chickens. Eggs were important on every farm for two reasons. They were an important part of the farm family's meals. In addition, farm women sold eggs to merchants in nearby towns, saying, "egg money is grocery money." With what she got for the eggs, the farm wife bought grocery items, like sugar and spices, she could not raise on the farm.

to be beaten and aired. Then the women put fresh padding (straw or newspaper) on the floors and tacked the carpets down again. Curtains were washed, starched, and stretched on frames.

Farm women also had to plan and start their gardens each spring. Big gardens provided much of the food for farm families. The gardens contained the same vegetables as pioneer gardens, plus tomatoes. Potatoes still took up the most space. New fruit trees might be planted, especially apple trees. During the summer women and children spent hours weeding and watering the gardens. Throughout the season, fruit and vegetables had to be picked and preserved. The root cellar was used less as women began to can vegetables and fruit in mason jars.

Some work was the same throughout the entire year. Many women helped milk eight to ten cows each day. After the milking, they had the task of putting the milk through the cream separator. Milk was poured into the top of the machine as someone turned the handle, sending skim milk out of one spout and cream out of another. Farm families consumed large quantities of milk, but the cream was sold or used to make butter and cheese. The skimmed milk was often fed to the pigs.

With their large gardens, chickens, and milk, farm families around 1900 were almost self-sufficient. That is, they produced their own food and bought only a few items at the local stores, such as coffee, flour, sugar, and salt.

Farm children also had regular tasks. As in pioneer days, boys helped their fathers with outdoor work— plowing, planting, and fixing fences. Girls worked with their mothers, often taking care of younger brothers and sisters. Daughters also helped prepare meals, wash dishes, and look after the chickens. In this way farm sons and daughters learned how to operate a farm and care for a farm family.

Farm children sometimes had to stay home from school to help their parents. On Monday, which was usually washday, the oldest daughters often helped with the laundry. Oldest sons frequently missed school in the fall to help pick corn and again in the spring to help with the planting. Children's labor was important on farms, and many parents believed that farmwork was more important than schoolwork.

There were some tasks on the farm that required everyone's help. Before World War II (1941–1945), most families did not have their own threshing machines but instead shared one with several other families. This arrangement was called a threshing ring.

We had a cider press and in season had gallons of fresh apple cider . . . No attempt was made to cut out the worms.
—Clifford Drury (around 1906)

State Historical Society

Threshing day on an Iowa farm in 1894.

The threshing ring had several advantages. First, each family did not have the expense of buying and keeping up their own machine. Instead, the cost was shared by five or six families. Second, at harvest time each family helped the others harvest their grain, so no one had to hire extra workers.

Threshing day was an exciting time on Iowa farms. The men began to arrive early in the morning, and the first task was to fire up the engine on the threshing rig. The fire heated the boiler filled with water, and that produced steam. Once the boiler was hot, the machine was ready for action.

Each man had certain duties. One man kept shoveling coal into the fire to keep up the steam. Other men pitched bundles of grain onto the wagons. Several men then drove the wagons to the threshing machine where the bundles of grain were pitched into it. The thresher separated the kernels of the barley or oat plant from the stalk. Because the work was done in August, it was usually very hot and humid. By the end of the day, the men were hot and tired from their work and sticky from all the straw chaff blown around by the machine.

Farm women helped with the threshing by preparing food for the workers. Threshing crews often spent two days at each farm so the women had several meals to prepare for a crew of ten to fifteen men. The noon meal was the big meal of the day and the women generally served several kinds of meat, vegetables, and pies along with huge quantities of potatoes and bread. On top of that, the women took an afternoon lunch out to the workers in the field.

At threshing time, farm families felt the farm was on display to the visiting workers. Each family tried to have their farm cleaned up so it would make a good impression on the visitors.

SOCIAL LIFE

Before 1900, farm families were quite isolated. In good weather they might travel to town about once a

208

week, but they left the farm far less often during the winter months. Even in warm weather, rain made the roads muddy, so the family often had to stay home. Because most farm roads were dirt before the 1930s, farm families had to plan their social activities and trips to town around the weather.

Social activities took place on the farm and involved mostly other family members. Brothers and sisters or cousins who lived nearby played games together. One man who grew up on a farm in Webster County remembered that he often had animals, such as colts, to play with.

On Iowa farms, relatives got together to celebrate birthdays and special holidays like Thanksgiving and Christmas. Often cousins saw each other at school and church, as well. Many churches and schools were located in the country, only a few miles from home.

In rural neighborhoods, schools were important not only for education, but also as places to hold social events. Country teachers and their students worked hard to prepare special programs. At Christmas, the students put on a performance for everyone in the area. They sang songs and acted out skits and plays. Another special time was in May when everyone came for a picnic to celebrate the end of the school year.

Sometimes country schools held box socials. At these events, each mother and daughter brought a separate lunch in a decorated box. Someone acted as an auctioneer, and the boxes were auctioned off to the men and boys. The highest bidder won the box and then ate with the person who had fixed it. Money raised by the box socials often went to fix up the school or buy additional pieces of equipment.

Farm families also took part in other social activities. Hamlin Garland wrote about his farm childhood in northern Iowa in the late 1880s. In his book, *Boy Life on the Prairie,* Garland described two main social events, the Fourth of July and the circus. At that time, every town in Iowa had a Fourth of July celebration with a parade, a ball game, and speeches by local officials. Garland's father took the entire family to the circus and Garland remembered this event with much happiness. He also remembered that when he went to town, he almost always got into a fight with town boys.

Advertisement for a circus at Iowa Falls around 1900.

State Historical Society

FARM LIFE IN THE EARLY TWENTIETH CENTURY

Around 1900, several important changes took place on Iowa farms. One was that the federal government began to deliver mail to each farm home. This was called Rural Free Delivery (RFD), which was a pleasant change from having to go to town to pick up mail. With RFD, letters, newspapers, and magazines could be delivered

210

each day. Daily newspapers meant that farmers could be better informed on market prices for their corn and hogs.

About the same time as RFD, farm families began to own new inventions. By 1900, many farm homes had telephones. A few years later, families began to buy automobiles. One farmer who grew up in the 1920s and 1930s remembered that farm people thought the automobile had been invented just for them! During the 1920s, rural people could buy battery-powered radios. By the 1930s, the radios were run by electricity, and the farm people could listen to market reports as well as music, plays, and other entertainment.

But even with cars and radios, farm people lived differently from town people. In the country, people could use their cars in good weather, but when it rained, they had to stay at home. In 1921, sixteen-year-old Helen Brainard, a farm girl from Casey, started her daily diary entry by describing the weather. Rain on dirt roads

211

meant she could not go to town, nor visit friends, and the mailman could not make his rounds.

Once farm homes got electricity and daily mail deliveries, farmers followed the market reports on the radio and in the newspaper.

Although farm people could travel more in the 1920s than before, other parts of farm life had not changed. They still labored from early morning until late at night. Most farmers still farmed with horses and put in long hours planting and harvesting their crops. Farm wives still raised large gardens, canning the vegetables and fruit. Families still butchered every year, and continued to raise chickens and milk cows.

Washing clothes remained the hardest job for farm women. Some women scrubbed all the laundry on a scrub board, including clothing, sheets, and towels. Others had hand-powered washing machines, but someone still had to push the lever back and forth for several hours to turn the paddles. By 1915, a few farm women were using Maytag washing machines, which were run by gasoline engines. They made washday far more pleasant.

By the 1920s, many people had become unhappy with farm life. The price of farm products had gone down, yet town people seemed to be making more money. Farm families felt they were not being rewarded for all their hard work. They were also unhappy that their homes did not have the comforts of town homes, such as electricity and bathrooms. Some people living in town had furnaces that heated the entire house evenly. Most farm people did not have electricity and did not have running water in the house. Every day someone had to carry in buckets of water from an outside well.

Some families became so unhappy with farming that they urged their older children to leave the farm. Women, especially, thought their children could find better and easier jobs in town. In the 1920s many young people did leave the farm. Some went to college and others found jobs in stores and factories in nearby cities and towns.

EXTENSION IN IOWA

During the first ten years of the twentieth century, the Iowa State Extension Service was started for farm families. The Extension Service's goals were to improve rural life. County agents, who had studied agriculture at Iowa State College (now Iowa State University), taught farmers ways to increase their corn yields or raise larger litters of pigs. County agents spread information on building better barns and chicken coops and on dealing with weeds and insects.

The Corn Belt stretches from eastern Nebraska through Iowa and Illinois to Indiana. Where tall prairie grass once grew, today row after row of corn grows in neatly plowed, square fields. Corn grows well in grasslands because it is really a giant member of the grass family. The leaves of corn even look like huge blades of grass.

Scientists believe that corn first grew in Mexico and Central America, though it did not look like modern corn. In some natural varieties each kernel was covered in its own pod and in others the ears were very small. Indians living in Mexico were the first to begin planting corn in gardens. They learned that the kernels were good to eat and very nutritious. As these people moved north, they took corn with them. Gradually, these groups migrated up the Mississippi River, growing corn in the rich soil along the rivers.

American Indians were growing corn in Iowa for hundreds of years before they met the first European

Perry Holden's seed corn "Gospel Train." Holden gives a lecture on growing better corn to Iowa farmers in the early 1900s.

Iowa State University

214

explorers and traders. In the spring, the Indians dug up pits where corn had been stored through the winter. Elderly women of the tribe carefully looked over the kernels. Only the largest and best seeds were saved for planting. Through this process of careful seed selection, the Indians slowly produced better and better varieties of corn. Over the years, the ears on the plants became larger, and there were more kernels on each ear.

American settlers in the new state of Iowa also planted corn and became interested in growing bigger and better corn plants. Perry Holden, a corn scientist at Iowa State College, urged farmers to examine their corn and to select only the very best seed for planting. All across the state, Holden held corn shows to tell farmers how to choose the best seeds to plant.

Henry A. Wallace also studied corn-growing at Iowa State. He studied how corn produces new plants. Developing one ear of corn involves two parts of the corn plant—the pollen in the tassel at the very top of the plant and the silks on the side of the plant where the ear will appear. The pollen falls from the tassel and fertilizes the corn silks. This causes the silks to begin developing into kernels on the ear of corn.

Wallace began experimenting. By taking the pollen from one variety to fertilize the silks of another variety, Wallace was able to develop new kinds of corn called hybrids. Wallace kept experimenting to develop better and better varieties. Ears grew longer, kernels grew larger, and the plants were stronger and resisted disease better. Wallace entered his hybrids in corn-growing contests all over the state. As the hybrids produced more corn in contest after contest, farmers wanted to plant the hybrids from Wallace's Pioneer Seed Corn Company in their fields. The development of hybrid seed greatly increased corn production throughout the Corn Belt.

Henry Agard Wallace, Secretary of Agriculture (1933–1941) and Vice President of the United States (1941–1945).

215

Extension home economists, who had studied ways to improve farm living, showed farm women how to prepare more nutritious meals and how to improve their sewing. Farm women also learned about home decoration, new fashions, and even how to make more attractive hats. For farm women, extension meetings also provided an important social time. It allowed women to get together with their neighbors and to talk about common problems.

Extension also provided 4-H programs for farm young people. In Iowa, Jessie Field Shambaugh started the first 4-H clubs. When she taught country school in Page County in southwestern Iowa, Mrs. Shambaugh realized that many farm children were ashamed that they lived on farms. She worried about this because she believed that farm people should take pride in the fact that they lived on farms. So she started clubs for both the boys and girls in her school. She believed that young people could be better prepared to farm if they studied more about farm life. In her school, boys learned about better farming methods and girls learned about keeping a farm home.

Later, Mrs. Shambaugh became the county superintendent of schools in Page county. A part of her job was to travel by horse and buggy all around the county, visiting every county school. In every school she visited, she knew each student by name and made sure that they could study agriculture. Visitors from all over the Midwest began to arrive in Page County to see for themselves what Mrs. Shambaugh had done.

In 1912, Mrs. Shambaugh started 4-H clubs for the whole state, with the goals of educating farm young people and instilling pride in their rural way of life. Both girls and boys joined 4-H clubs and their parents served as leaders. Before long, clubs began to appear in other states.

The highlight of the year for 4-H'ers was the end of summer when it was time for the county fair. By then, they had raised their gardens and animals and had finished their special projects. A trip to the county fair gave them a chance to exhibit their work. The winners of the first prizes were allowed to take their projects to the state fair.

FARM LIFE IN THE 1930s

Farm families had many difficulties in the 1920s and then faced even greater problems in the 1930s. During that decade, the entire nation was going through the Great Depression. The price of farm products dropped sharply. Although farm families usually managed to raise enough food to eat, they had little money to spend. Many families had mortgages (loans to repay) on their farms, and during the 1930s some of these families could not keep up the payments and lost their farms.

Even though times were hard, some good things did happen during the Depression. In 1935, the federal government set up the Rural Electrification Association (REA), which brought electricity to farm homes. For the first time, most farm families could have electric lights and water could be pumped, instead of carried, into the farmhouse. Farm women could have electric appliances like stoves and refrigerators. One farm woman rejoiced that electricity was like having many servants. For the first time, farm families could have the same comforts as town families.

Another important change in the 1930s was that many country roads were paved. Most farm families had bought cars during the 1920s. Now with better roads, they could get to town more often, and they could take vacations. Better roads made farm life more enjoyable for all family members.

During the 1920s and 1930s, farmers changed some of their farming methods. In 1900, every Iowa farmer used horses for power, but by 1920, some farmers had purchased tractors and more bought them during the 1930s. A few farmers continued to use horses because they thought tractors were too expensive, or just because they liked having the horses around the farm.

Today there are far fewer farms in Iowa than in the 1920s and 1930s, but of course many families still live on farms and farming is still the biggest business in the state. Iowans take great pride in agriculture. Farm people feel today, as they did in 1900 and 1930, that the farm is a good place to live and to raise children. On a farm, young people learn to work hard and to accept responsibility. An important change, however, is that today's farm families have homes and belongings as modern as those of families living in towns and cities.

FURTHER READING

Bonney, Margaret, ed. "Come to the Fair!" *The Goldfinch* 5, no. 1 (September 1983). Iowa City: State Historical Society of Iowa.

Graber, William Bernard. "A Farm Family Enters the Modern World." *The Palimpsest* 68, no. 2 (Summer 1987). Iowa City: State Historical Society of Iowa.

Salvaneschi, Lenore. "Harvest Time." *The Palimpsest* 65, no. 6 (November/December 1984). Iowa City: State Historical Society of Iowa.

14 New Inventions Bring Change

Within the past century, new inventions have made a huge difference in the lives of Iowa families. Telephones and automobiles completely changed communication and transportation. Modern families visit friends hundreds of miles away more easily than Iowa pioneers could travel to a nearby town. Electricity changed many ways Iowans do things at home and at work. Electric lights made homes cleaner and brighter when they replaced the old lamps that burned kerosene. Electric appliances that we hardly notice today, like vacuum cleaners and washing machines, do away with the incredible drudgery of housework in earlier days.

TELEPHONES

On March 10, 1876, Alexander Graham Bell made the first telephone call in history. That summer, Bell displayed his new machine at an exhibition in Philadelphia in honor of the 100th birthday of the United States. Thousands of impressed visitors shouted into a small box to send their voices through the wire.

> Mr. Watson, come here, I want you.
> —Alexander Graham Bell (first telephone call, 1876)

People quickly realized how useful telephones could be. A wealthy Des Moines businessman, Frederick M. Hubbell, ran a telephone line from his home to his office. The fire stations in Burlington rigged up telephones with each other to speed reports of fires and other emergencies. In many towns, hotels strung telephone lines to the railroad station so drivers would not waste time waiting for late trains. When the train came in, someone at the station called the hotel to send a buggy to pick up the passengers.

At first, every pair of telephones was connected by its own wire, which was strung along housetops, barns, and trees – anything to keep it high off the ground. From the phone in his home, Mr. Hubbell could speak only with someone at his office. He could not call anyone else in Des Moines, which limited the early use of the new invention.

Before long, telephone companies were formed to install phones in homes and businesses and to connect all the lines into a common switchboard. A telephone operator sat at the switchboard and took calls. The caller told the operator the name or number of the person to be called, and the operator then connected the lines of the two phones. With the switchboard system, any caller could reach any other telephone connected to the system.

The telephone switchboard operator became a central person in town life.

In smaller towns, the telephone operator did more than just connect phone calls. In case of a fire, people called the operator and she sounded the alarm. (Curious townsfolk even called the operator to find out where the fire was.) Operators located doctors in an emergency. People called her to ask the correct time of day. In small towns, residents came to rely on the operator for information.

Farm families also wanted telephone service, but it was harder and more expensive to install telephones in the country because of the distance between farm homes. To reduce costs, farm families often helped to put up the lines themselves. They formed companies called cooperatives (co-ops) in order to have phones. In a co-op, all the families using the services share expenses and run the company.

State Historical Society

Telephone crews busy stringing new lines in Jackson County in 1906.

When country telephone lines ran long distances, many families often connected their phones to the same line. Sometimes as many as twelve or fifteen homes shared such a "party line." When two people were talking, all the other families on the line could listen in. Often people joined in a neighborhood discussion, and there were many stories about people who shared secrets on the party line, forgetting that others might be quietly listening.

Telephones were a great help to farm families. Men could call each other for help with big jobs. Farm women, whose work kept them at home, especially enjoyed the new service to keep in touch with neighbors or nearby relatives. When someone was sick, the family could call a doctor. When snow blocked the roads, doctors gave instructions over the telephone—even on how to deliver babies!

In 1920, a farm in Iowa was more likely to have a telephone than a farm in any other state. Most Iowa families could call friends all over the state, and long-distance service permitted them to speak directly to people anywhere in the nation. The Bell Telephone Company, founded by the inventor, soon became the largest business company in the United States.

AUTOMOBILES

Around 1900, several different inventors tried to build "horseless carriages," but the first autos did not work well. They were so heavy that they often got stuck in mud. The engines broke down, and they were loud, hard to steer, and very expensive. In 1900, some models cost $6,000 or $7,000, which was as much as a farm and four or five times more than many men earned in a whole year. So only wealthy families could afford automobiles.

Keeping your hat from blowing away was important in the early automobiles.

> **My father bought a beautiful, big, red, seven-passenger Sterling. It got stuck any time we went any place. It was a lemon, you know, what you get once in a while.**
>
> **—Bess Osgood (Jefferson, 1900s)**

While people enjoyed taking short rides for fun, few thought that cars would ever replace horses. People then did not travel as much as they do today. For example, in 1910 Roy Mosteller, a farm boy who lived north of Scranton, used to make the seven-mile trip from Scranton to Jefferson with his mother to visit relatives. On the day of the trip, they got up early, ate breakfast, hitched up a horse to their buggy, and drove the three miles into Scranton. There Roy put the horse in a livery stable and Mrs. Mosteller bought tickets on the 8:00 train for Jefferson. After shopping and visiting all day, they returned on an evening train to Scranton, where they got back in their buggy and arrived home in time for a late supper. Because such trips of ten miles required careful planning, the Mostellers limited them to four or five a year.

Several years later, the Mosteller family bought an automobile, in which they could make the whole trip in twenty to thirty minutes. More and more Iowans discovered how useful a car could be.

223

The Most Satisfactory Investment
for the Country Physician
by Harry P. Engle, M.D., Newton, Iowa

When I purchased an automobile I had had no experience with machinery of any kind, and knew practically nothing concerning the principles of a gas engine.

My three years' experience in a motorcar has been with a single-cylinder, 9-horsepower, water-cooled gasoline machine. I have taken care of it myself. I have averaged over 3,000 miles each year and have found the cost of driving a motorcar to be less than keeping a team, and the comfort, convenience and pleasure place the automobile so far ahead that I never expect to own another horse. I have driven the machine at all times of the year, over all kinds of roads. With the patent chain tire grips for mud and ice and calcium chloride for zero temperature you can always be sure of getting back home.

After driving the car about six months I sold my horses, but when the roads are very bad I depend on the livery, preferring, as I did when I owned a team, to drive the livery horses over the worst roads. Mrs. Engle is also an automobile enthusiast and handles the car with perfect ease, starting the engine without difficulty, and I feel sure that everything will be all right when she is out driving.

Ninety-five per cent of all my trouble has been with the pneumatic tires. A medical friend tells me that he has completely solved this problem by using solid rubber on his machine, and that the solid tires do not (as claimed by pneumatic people) jar the machine to pieces. I have concluded to try them when in need of new tires.

There is no question about the usefulness of an automobile to a physician. It is so much quicker and can be left standing anywhere without an attendant. It can easily cover twice the ground in a day that a horse can, and in the summer, when the warm weather is hard on a horse, the auto is a great advantage, as both machine and driver are cooler when going fast. (*Journal of the American Medical Association,* 1906)

An early automobile in Iowa around 1912.

When cars became more dependable and less expensive, many families bought them. They found that cars were better than a horse and buggy in many ways. Cars could travel long distances while horses needed rest and daily care even when they were not being used. Most important, automobiles traveled faster. Because trips did not take as much time, families traveled much more when they owned a car.

At first, there were no laws about who could drive. Children, some as young as eleven or twelve, were allowed to practice on country roads although most were older before they began driving. When the state passed a law that required all drivers to get a license, children could not drive legally until they were teenagers.

Reliability and low cost.

—Slogan for Ford Model T car

225

In 1908, there was a new car for sale, the Model T Ford. Its designer, Henry Ford, wanted to make a car that ordinary families could own. It had to be inexpensive, dependable, and easy to operate. The Model T was all of these, and the "Tin Lizzie," as it was called, became the most popular car in America.

The Model T was not expensive. At first, it cost around $900, but the price later dropped to $250. Because Ford made millions of the same model, he was able to cut his costs of production and charge a lower price for each one. Ford brought all the parts to his factory in Detroit, Michigan, where workers on an assembly line put the cars together. Because each worker did only one job on each vehicle, the cars moved rapidly through the line. They all looked alike. Ford said that his customers could have any color car they wanted, "so long as it's black."

The Model T was dependable. It did not get stuck in the mud as often as heavier cars. If it broke down, it was easy to repair, and drivers learned how to fix its simple engine and change flat tires. Owners could buy new parts in most cities and towns.

It was not hard to drive. Its top speed was around thirty miles an hour, and it was easy to steer. For thousands of American families, the Model T was the first car they ever owned.

Automobiles led to many changes for Iowans. As more people began driving, they wanted better roads. Iowa country roads became muddy in spring, and early cars often got stuck. Dirt roads were bumpy and dusty in summer and fall and often blocked by deep snow in the winter. Farm families needed good roads to get into town, and everyone wanted good roads when they drove to visit other towns.

State Historical Society

Early drivers had a hard time in Iowa because the roads were poor.

Better roads cost money. It took money to buy gravel and to pay workers to spread it on the roads. To help pay for better roads, the state government put a tax on gasoline. Drivers paid a few cents more for a gallon of gasoline to provide money for a road fund. Those who drove the most bought the most gasoline and paid the most to make the roads better.

At first, it was hard to drive from one town to another because there were no highway or road signs. Drivers had to ask local people for directions and often became lost in the countryside. In a few places there were markers on fences or telephone poles, but not on most roads. To help drivers find their way, the government put up signs and printed road maps.

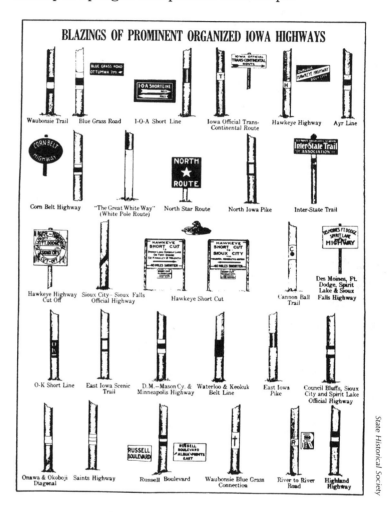

BLAZINGS OF PROMINENT ORGANIZED IOWA HIGHWAYS

Waubonsie Trail · Blue Grass Road · I-O-A Short Line · Iowa Official Trans-Continental Route · Hawkeye Highway · Ayr Line

Corn Belt Highway · "The Great White Way" (White Pole Route) · North Star Route · North Iowa Pike · Inter-State Trail

Hawkeye Highway Cut Off · Sioux City–Sioux Falls Official Highway · Hawkeye Short Cut · Cannon Ball Trail · Des Moines, Ft. Dodge, Spirit Lake & Sioux Falls Highway

O-K Short Line · East Iowa Scenic Trail · D.M.–Mason Cy. & Minneapolis Highway · Waterloo & Keokuk Belt Line · East Iowa Pike · Council Bluffs, Sioux City and Spirit Lake Official Highway

Onawa & Okoboji Diagonal · Saints Highway · Russell Boulevard · Waubonsie Blue Grass Connection · River to River Road · Highland Highway

Before highways were clearly marked, travelers had to read all kinds of road signs.

Families began taking long trips in their cars, including summer vacations. Before automobiles, trips were expensive. Travelers had to buy train tickets for the whole family and sleep in hotels or pay for sleeping cars on the train. With cars, families could camp along the way and cook their meals over campfires, instead of eating in restaurants. Since camping was cheap, families were able to see more of the country. Many towns provided parks or camping areas for travelers. Soon Iowa families were visiting new places. Yellowstone Park became popular, and Lake Okoboji and Spirit Lake in northwest Iowa attracted thousands of tourists. Small parks all over the state had more and more visitors.

Automobiles made it possible for many families to spend a week camping at the Iowa State Fair.

New businesses sprang up to take care of the travelers. The word "motel" was created to mean a motorist's hotel. The first motels often were little cabins built along the road for traveling families. Service stations sold gasoline and repaired automobiles. Roadside cafes opened up along well-traveled routes.

At the same time, however, other businesses began to disappear. As more families bought automobiles, there was less need for horses. Most Iowa towns once had several livery stables where horses were kept and fed. As automobiles replaced horses, most of the livery stables closed. Blacksmiths who fitted horses with horseshoes had less to do, and many went into other types of work. Merchants who had sold buggies began selling automobiles or shifted into some other new product. Fewer people traveled on the train, so railroads became less important. Today, most railroads no longer even carry passengers. They haul only freight.

State Historical Society

A parade of automobiles at Everly, Iowa, probably around the end of World War I.

Automobiles brought important changes for the country school. Before cars, there were many small schools for farm children. Most families lived within one or two miles of a schoolhouse, and the children walked there. One teacher taught all students through the eighth grade in the same classroom. As more farm families bought automobiles, the small country schools began to close because farm children could travel to larger schools in town. Before cars, most farm children did not attend high school, since there were few high schools in the country. The farm children who wanted to attend high school had to live in town through the week and go home only on weekends. When automobiles shortened the daily trip, more farm children took high school classes.

School districts began sending out buses to pick up farm children who wanted to attend classes in town. Early school buses were often trucks with wooden sides built on the back and long benches along the sides. They rarely had heaters. In the winter, students wrapped up in blankets and put their feet on hot bricks that their

230

parents had heated in the stove.

Automobiles brought other changes. People could travel faster and more easily with cars than with horses, so they traveled more and learned about the world outside their own communities. In fact, the coming of the automobile is one of the most important changes in the past one hundred years.

ELECTRICITY

In 1882, Thomas Edison, one of America's greatest inventors, built generators that produced large quantities of electricity. The first generating plant in the United States was built in New York City. Other cities and towns copied the idea. In some Iowa cities, the local governments built the plants and sold electricity to the townspeople. In other communities, private companies owned and operated the electric plants. They strung the electric wires from house to house, and before long, families in Iowa towns were enjoying the wonders of the new service.

Lights were normally the first electrical item a family added. Before electricity, most homes had been lighted by lamps that burned kerosene, which comes from oil. As the kerosene burned and the lamp gave off light, the glass chimney over the burning wick became black with soot. It had to be washed regularly, or the soot would shut out the light.

Electric lights were much brighter than kerosene lamps. One little girl, Alice Ann Thompson, did not like to go to homes where there were electric lights. Her mother believed that dirt showed up more under electric lights and made her scrub her face and wash behind her ears whenever they visited a home with electricity.

Mother believed that dirt showed up more under electric lights. She made me scrub my face hard and wash behind my ears whenever we visited a house with electricity.
—Alice Thompson (Jefferson, 1978)

231

Towns and cities began placing electric lights on the street to make the street crossings and sidewalks safer at night.

THE DREARIEST OF DREARY EARLY SPRING DAYS WAS WASH DAY IN OUR STEAMY KITCHEN THAT SMELLED OF LAUNDRY SOAP AND BOILED CABBAGE — IT SEEMED A BOILED CABBAGE DINNER WAS PART OF WASH DAY.

MOM, I'LL SURE BE GLAD WHEN WE HAVE NICE SUNNY DAYS SO WE CAN WASH OUT IN THE YARD UNDER THE EVERGREEN TREE

BUT YOU DON'T LIKE WASH DAY THEN EITHER

Families soon added other electrical items to their homes. Many women were happy to try electric irons on their clothes. Before the electric iron, heavy "sadirons" had to be heated on the stove. Then the woman lifted one of them to the ironing board and used it to smooth out wrinkles until it cooled. She placed it back on the stove and picked up a fresh hot iron while the first one reheated. Ironing was hard work because the irons were heavy and the stove was hot. An electric iron was much lighter, and the user could move the ironing board into a cooler room. Women liked them very much, and their sales grew rapidly.

Other electric appliances also made housekeeping easier. Vacuum sweepers cleaned rugs more thoroughly. Toasters simplified making breakfast. Refrigerators kept milk, eggs, butter, and other food cool, while washing machines took much of the hard work out of washing dirty clothes. Radios provided hours of entertainment.

232

Farm families wanted these conveniences but were not able to have electrical service as early as town families. It cost too much to put up the miles of electrical lines to reach rural homes. Because farm families had to wait many years for electricity, farm homes took much more work to care for than town homes. Rural families had to carry water in buckets from an outside pump. With no refrigerators, they stored food in the cellar or a well to keep it from spoiling. Most homes did not have indoor bathrooms. Farm families had to heat water on the stove for their baths and dishwater. Electricity made a big difference between town homes and farm homes.

In 1935, the U.S. government began to help farm families get electricity. It loaned money to groups of farmers to build electric lines in the country, and within ten years rural families were enjoying the comfort and convenience of electrical appliances. Farmers found many uses for electric power. They purchased electric milking machines, put in electric pumps to provide drinking water for their livestock, and installed electric heaters to keep the chickenhouse warm in the winter. Farmers were soon using more electricity than most townspeople.

As Iowans began to demand more electric power, new ways of making electricity had to be found. At first, each city or town had its own generating plant, but these were often too small to meet the growing demands for the new power. Electric companies built huge new electric generators to furnish electricity for a large area. Most of these plants burned coal to produce steam to turn the generators. Near Cedar Rapids, one company has built an atomic power plant to produce electricity. The Duane Arnold plant began operating in 1974.

An Iowan helped to develop an exciting new use for electricity—computers.

> The electric iron was *the* greatest drudgery-saver ever invented.
> —Myrtle Morain (housewife, Jefferson, 1978)

John Vincent Atanasoff, inventor of the computer, in his Maryland workshop, 1967.

In 1938 John Vincent Atanasoff, a scientist at Iowa State University, wanted to invent a machine that could do very difficult mathematics problems. People had been trying to make one for centuries. The Chinese used rows of beads on an abacus to do large calculations quickly. In 1642, a Frenchman named Blaise Pascal built a machine to do simple arithmetic problems.

Using some of the ideas of earlier models, Atanasoff tried to make a better calculating machine. One evening he was in his office, thinking hard about how to design his new machine. Nothing seemed to work. Discouraged, he decided to forget the project for a while and go for a drive to clear his mind. Atanasoff later recalled: "Every once in a while I would commence to think about my efforts to build a computer and I didn't want to do that so I would drive harder so I could not think. . . . When I finally came to earth, I was crossing the Mississippi river, 189 miles from my desk."

Atanasoff stopped his car, went into a roadside cafe, and sat down. Suddenly his mind became clear and sharp. He recalled: "I knew what I wanted to think about and I went right to work on it and worked for three hours. Then I got in my car and drove slowly back to Ames."

At the table in the cafe, Atanasoff had worked out some ideas that helped create the modern computer. Earlier adding machines had gears and rods that "counted off" numbers as they were entered. Atanasoff decided to replace the gears with electrical equipment. Numbers could be entered as electrical impulses. It was a complicated plan, but Atanasoff believed it could work.

The university provided some money and a student assistant, Clifford E. Berry, to help Atanasoff build the actual model. Berry began working with Atanasoff on a small model in the fall of 1939. In a few weeks, they were making good progress in a basement workshop on the Iowa State campus. In early trial runs, the model worked well, and so Atanasoff and Berry began work on a full-scale model. Then World War II began and both men left Ames in 1942 to take government jobs. Their computing machine was stored away and forgotten at Iowa State.

In the 1950s, other people working on computers discovered what Atanasoff and Berry had done before the war. Atanasoff had developed the first modern computer at Iowa State University. Although neither of them collected any money for the invention, Atanasoff wrote, "I am very grateful that fate should have placed me at the beginning of this great adventure."

New inventions have brought many changes to Iowa towns and farms. Things that seem common today were exciting inventions a hundred years ago. The telephone has made it possible to talk to people far away. Automobiles greatly aided travel, which in turn brought business and social change. More than anything else, electricity has changed the way we live. Farm, town, or city— electricity made homes and farms more comfortable and efficient.

FURTHER READING

Bonney, Margaret, ed. "The Sky's the Limit." *The Goldfinch* 2, no. 1 (September 1980). Iowa City: State Historical Society of Iowa.

———, ed. "The Automobile Age." *The Goldfinch* 4, no. 2. (November 1982). Iowa City: State Historical Society of Iowa.

Engle, Harry P., M.D. "The Most Satisfactory Investment for the Country Physician." *The Goldfinch,* Margaret Bonney, ed. 4, no. 2 (November 1982). Reprinted from the *Journal of the American Medical Association,* 1906. Iowa City: State Historical Society of Iowa.

Pittman, Von V., Jr. "Station WSUI and the Early Days of Instructional Radio." *The Palimpsest* 67, no. (March/April 1986). Iowa City: State Historical Society of Iowa.

15   Business and Industry in Iowa

Iowans manufacture (make) many different products, including tractors, washing machines, and ballpoint pens. The companies that make products like these are called industries, and the buildings where they are made are called factories. The first products manufactured in our state were made within the home in the 1800s. Factories appeared later.

Through the years, Iowa industries have been related to agriculture, using the corn, oats, beef, and pork raised on Iowa farms. Most Iowa industries have been located in the eastern part of the state, which has the largest cities to provide the work force. Iowa products are sold all over the world.

BUSINESS AND INDUSTRY, 1833–1870

Even before factories were built in our state, products were made on the farm, usually related to farming. A farmer might make a harness for his horse or cut down trees and saw lumber to build houses and barns. As a rule, manufacturing was winter work when farmers did not have to be in the fields.

Before long, separate business places developed in the state. One of the first was a gristmill that ground wheat or corn into flour. Farmers brought their grain from miles away and often had to wait several days for their turn. They usually paid the miller by giving him part of the flour, because farmers in the mid-1800s had little money.

Lumber Industry

As people settled along the Mississippi River in the 1830s and 1840s, the need for timber to build homes and businesses led to the growth of a lumber industry. At first, it was simple to hire workers to cut down the trees along the river and saw them into boards. Before long, however, most of the trees had been cut down along the Iowa stretch of the Mississippi, so Iowa lumbermen had to bring logs down the river from Wisconsin.

Workers planing and sawing lumber. In the mid-1800s many Iowa towns along the Mississippi had sawmills to process Iowa and Wisconsin timber.

237

Workers transporting logs to a nearby sawmill on a horse-pulled sleigh.

A steamboat moving logs down the Mississippi River.

Logs stacked for processing at a Mississippi River city. The buildings with the smokestacks are sawmills.

The Fleming sawmill at Marquette.

A store and workshop in Dubuque where lumber was made into items such as door frames, window sashes, and cabinets.

239

General Stores

As more settlers arrived, more businesses appeared. One of the first was the general store with a little bit of everything but not much of anything. Early Iowans shopped in these stores for both their family and their animals.

Many early storekeepers, such as Charles Brewster, developed more than one business. Brewster was born in Ireland and immigrated to the United States when he was twelve years old. As a young man, he opened a dry goods (fabric and clothing) store in Fort Madison that he operated for thirty years. Brewster was really a general merchant who sold cloth by the bolt, ready-made clothing (such as overalls, hats, and shoes), patent medicines, and cigars and tobacco, as well as hardware products and dishes.

As a part of his store, Brewster developed smaller lines of business. He bought eggs, butter, and meat from nearby farm families. Some he sold to townspeople in Fort Madison, but most were shipped to eastern cities. Brewster also loaned money to customers, bought land

The milliner in her shop at Richland, Iowa.

State Historical Society

While most businesses were operated by men, women also owned stores. During the nineteenth and early twentieth centuries, Iowa towns, large and small, had millinery shops that sold hats. In 1880, for example, Greenfield had a total of 684 people and seven milliners. Iowa Falls had almost 1,000 people in 1880 and four milliners. These were important businesses at a time when women believed that they always needed to wear a hat or bonnet. The milliners (almost always women) made new hats and redecorated old ones.

The milliner was a respected business person. The *Iowa State Register* in 1878 wrote about Mrs. M. M. Clark, who owned a millinery shop in Des Moines and whose fame was due to

> her exquisite taste in adapting a hat or bonnet to the peculiar style of the wearer. In millinery this is everything, for the handsomest bonnet loses its character if not adapted to the wearer with cunning ingenuity. . . . Just in what this mysterious adaptation consists of takes an accomplished milliner to tell.

The millinery shop provided women with a place to meet. In most towns men had places to gather, such as the barber shop, livery stable, and pool hall, where women felt out of place. In a millinery shop, women could chat and pick out ribbons and flowers to decorate their hats. Edith Jacks, a milliner in the 1880s, recalled,

> Milliners then did not have a six-hour day; often in the busy seasons their work began at six a.m., extending until nine or ten o'clock at night.

The milliner herself had an interesting job. Often she traveled to large cities to buy her supplies. There she could learn about new fashions and share this news with her customers back home. Mrs. C. G. Jones, milliner at the East Algona Ladies' Emporium, placed this advertisement in the local Algona newspaper in the late nineteenth century.

> Lively and faithful illustrations of the Latest Fashions constantly on exhibition including trimmed samples of Ladies and Childrens Wear direct from New York. All requisite information of the kind, quantity, and quality of material and the proper style of making up all kinds of Ladies' Wear given gratis [free].

In the nineteenth century, most Iowans did not believe that women should own businesses or have careers of their own, but no one seemed to argue with the idea that women could make and sell hats. For many women, owning a millinery shop provided a good living and a chance to develop their own business skills.

for people who lived in the East, and even wrote letters for those who could not read or write.

In 1875, Charles Brewster sold his general store in Fort Madison and started a bank there. After that, he had only the banking business.

INDUSTRIES AFTER 1870

By 1870, Iowa had four railroads that ran from the eastern border to the western border of the state. Products could then be shipped around and out of the state.

Because of this, railroads were extremely important to the development of industry in Iowa. Buttons made in Muscatine could be sent to San Francisco, and meat products from Ottumwa could be sent to New York. Better still, railroads operated every month of the year. Steamboats, which had been the most important type of transportation before 1870, could not operate during the winter when the rivers froze over. After 1870, many more industries developed in Iowa because of improved transportation.

Meat Packing

Meat packing was one of the new industries. In 1877, Thomas Foster came to the Midwest looking for a place to set up the John Morrell meat-packing plant. Foster looked at several cities and then decided that the plant should be built in Ottumwa for several reasons. First, the city had a good water supply. The Des Moines River flowed through it. Second, Ottumwa could provide enough men to work in the plant. Third, and perhaps the most important, Ottumwa had a railroad that would transport the meat products out to various markets.

Another reason why Foster chose Ottumwa was because Iowa farmers raised the cattle and hogs that the Morrell plant needed for its meat products. Since the animals were raised nearby, Morrell officials had to pay less for shipping the animals to the plant.

During the 1870s other Iowa cities also set up meat-packing plants. The Sinclair Meat Packing Company was constructed in Cedar Rapids. Sioux City soon became one of the most important meat-packing centers in Iowa as several different companies located there.

Quaker Oats

At the same time, other farm-related industries came to Iowa. One of these was Quaker Oats, which started in Cedar Rapids in 1873. John and Robert Stuart (father and son) and George Douglas (John's cousin) started the company. The Stuarts came from Canada and Douglas came from Scotland.

Before they came to Iowa, the Stuarts had manufactured oatmeal in Canada, but they thought they could make better oatmeal in Cedar Rapids. Mainly, the men believed that oats grew better in Iowa than in Canada. Other conditions were right. The Cedar River flowed through the city to provide water. Cedar Rapids also had plenty of people to work in the plant.

But the Stuarts and Douglas had one big problem. In the 1870s, most people did not eat oatmeal because they believed that it was not a food for humans — only horses ate oats. Oatmeal producers set out to convince Americans that oatmeal was good for them. They advertised their product all over the country as a cheap and wholesome food. Soon many Americans were buying oatmeal, and the largest plant was in Cedar Rapids, Iowa.

The Quaker Oats Company plant at Cedar Rapids around 1960.

State Historical Society

Deere & Company

In 1837 John Deere built a plow that worked well on the Illinois prairie. Farmers had complained because the rich, black prairie soil stuck to the moldboard (blade) of the plow. Then they had to stop their plowing and scrape off the sticky dirt with a paddle or stick. Deere, a blacksmith, came up with the idea of using smooth steel on the moldboard so that the plow would scour (remain clear). He set up a factory to sell his plows in Grand Detour, Illinois, but later moved to Moline. By the end of the century, the company had grown into a large corporation that sold machinery nationwide.

In 1918, Deere & Company bought a factory in Waterloo where they began to manufacture tractors. Not many farmers had tractors in 1918 but twenty years later most farmers owned one. Deere also manufactured many different farm implements, including plows, corn planters, cultivators, and harrows.

Today, Deere sells farm machinery all over the world. Although the company has its headquarters in Moline, Illinois, they do most of their manufacturing of farm equipment in Iowa. Deere & Company has factories in Dubuque, Ottumwa, Waterloo, and Ankeny, each manufacturing different machinery. In Ottumwa, for example, workers make lawn and garden equipment and self-propelled harvesters.

The Maytag Company

Not all Iowa industries were farm-related, however. The Maytag Company at Newton started making washing machines in 1909. Frederick Maytag, whose parents were German immigrants, attended school for only three years. Then he tried different types of work. Sometimes

> **Nothing runs like a Deere.**
> —Deere & Company (advertising slogan)

he made money, but sometimes he did not. At sixteen, he started a threshing machine operation for local farmers. After seven years Maytag decided to do something different. With money earned from threshing, he bought a team of horses to haul coal from a nearby coal mine to customers in Newton. Unfortunately, one of his horses fell and broke its leg, which ended the coal-hauling business.

A few years later, Maytag went into the farm implement business, first only as a salesman but soon becoming a part owner. He began to manufacture an attachment for threshing machines that fed the grain into the machine automatically, instead of by hand. Maytag's invention made the work faster and safer.

Another manufacturing interest of Maytag's was building automobiles. His main car was called the Maytag Hill Climber. The company put out five different models of the Hill Climber, called A, B, C, E, and F. Model A was called the "Farmer's Car" and sold for about $1,250. The rear seat could be taken out to carry farm products. Model F sold for $1,750 and was described as "big, powerful, elegant."

In 1909, Maytag started his most successful operation when he made an electric washing machine with a hand-operated wringer. A few years later, the Maytag Company put out a washing machine with a gasoline motor, which could be used on farms and in other homes that did not have electricity.

The Maytag Company came up with many new features for their machine, such as a rustproof aluminum tub that provided a smoother inside surface. Later, the company introduced an agitator attached to the bottom of the tub. On earlier machines the agitator, which is the part that swishes the clothes around inside the tub, had been attached to the lid and did not do a good job of

246

getting the clothes clean. By 1924, the Maytag Company was selling more washing machines than any other company in the entire country.

Later, the Maytag Company built clothes dryers and automatic dishwashers. From the beginning they have been known for the high quality of their products, which are now sold all over the world.

Pearl Buttons

In the late nineteenth century, people in Muscatine made pearl buttons. The material they used came from the Mississippi River in the form of clamshells.

The pearl button industry started by accident when John Boepple, a German immigrant, stepped on something sharp while taking a swim in the river. He picked it up and found that it looked much like clamshells he had seen used for pearl buttons in Germany. Boepple took some shells home to cut out buttons, which he promptly sold to a Muscatine merchant. Boepple's buttons were the first freshwater pearl buttons made in this country.

Boepple saw that there was a market for pearl buttons in Iowa so he built a machine to drag the river. It

Workers in a pearl button factory in Muscatine around 1900.

consisted of three-pronged hooks, called crowfeet, which he pulled over the river bottom to collect the clams. Later, Boepple built a machine to cut buttons out of the clamshells. The next step was to drill holes (for thread) and put a design or decoration on each button. Before long, more than forty button factories were operating in Muscatine. For years the pearl button industry was important in Muscatine, but too much fishing reduced the number of clams and the button factories dwindled away. The last four hung on until World War II, when the invention of plastic buttons drove them out of business. Today all the pearl button factories in Iowa have closed.

Coal Mining

Coal mining also used material found in Iowa—under the ground. The first mining started as early as the 1840s, when people discovered coal in the southeastern part of the state. The coal was burned only to heat homes and businesses but as the railroads arrived, coal was needed to provide steam power to run the trains. By 1880, there were more than two hundred coal mines operating in Iowa. Twenty years later, that number had increased to over four hundred. All these mines were underground (most were about 250 feet underground) and were called shaft mines.

Big Jim Coal Mine at Seymour in 1909. Many Italian-Americans worked at the Big Jim mine.

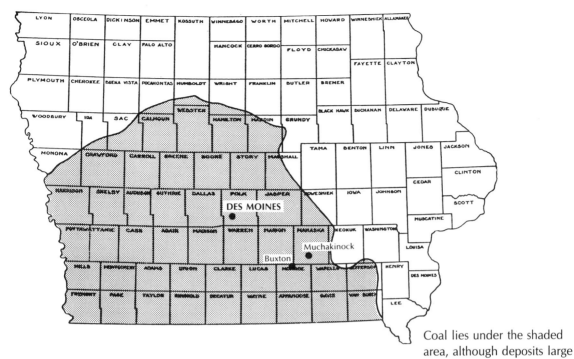

Coal lies under the shaded area, although deposits large enough to mine are mostly in the southern part.

Most coal deposits were some distance from towns, so coal companies had to build houses for the workers. These places were called coal camps. The coal company owned the town, employed all the workers, and made all the rules. Houses in the camps were small, usually four rooms. Since many families had four children or more, living conditions were crowded.

Most of the workers were miners, the men who dug the coal. But coal companies also needed men for other jobs, both above and under the ground. All workers other than miners were called "company men." The company men operated the elevator that brought the coal out of the ground and drove the mules that pulled the coal cars around underground. They also installed electricity underground and opened up new parts of the mines.

Working in a mine was dangerous. Often a piece of the slate roof fell on a miner, sometimes breaking an arm or leg. Sometimes it killed him. If the mules went too fast, the miner would be pinned between the wall and the coal cars. Mule drivers could fall under the wheels of the coal cars.

In Iowa, coal mining remained an important industry until the 1920s. Then Iowans began to buy coal from other states because they believed it was better. Railroads also began to buy coal in Illinois and Kentucky. Gradually, the coal mines shut down, until by the 1950s only about twenty mines were still operating. Today, there are only two underground mines in Iowa.

Iowans are still producing coal but they are mining it in a different way. There are about ten stripmines in the state. With stripmining, the dirt is peeled off the top and then huge machines scoop up the coal. Because the work is done on top of the ground, stripmining is safer than underground mining and also cheaper.

The five leading Iowa manufacturing and processing industries by year

Industry	Census Year							
	1870	1880	1890	1900	1910	1920	1930	1940
Flour and gristmill products	X	X		X				
Lumber	X	X	X	X	X			
Furniture	X							
Meat packing		X	X	X	X	X	X	X
Carpentry and building	X		X	X				
Woolen goods	X							
Carriages and wagons		X						
Blacksmithing		X						
Printing and publishing			X		X	X	X	X
Railroad cars, repairs, etc.			X	X	X	X		
Foundry and machine shop products					X	X	X	
Food preparation						X		
Household appliances							X	
Bread and bakery products							X	X
Corn syrup, sugar, oil, etc.								X
Planing mills not with sawmills								X

TWENTIETH-CENTURY MANUFACTURING

Sheaffer Pen Company

During the twentieth century, Iowans have started various industries. One was making fountain pens. In 1908, a jeweler in Bloomfield, Walter Sheaffer, repaired pens in his jewelry store. A common complaint was that pens leaked ink. Sheaffer decided that he could make a leak-proof fountain pen. He moved his business to Fort Madison where he began to manufacture different types of pens. Today the Sheaffer Company, known as the Sheaffer Eaton Company, manufactures pens, stationery, and other writing products.

Collins Radio Company

As a boy in Cedar Rapids, Arthur Collins was interested in radios. In 1918, he put together a crystal set, which was the first form of radio. His first radio transmitter was made from a Quaker Oats box, a wire from a Model T Ford, and telephone parts. In the 1930s, he set up a workshop in the basement of his home and, with his father's help, made parts for radios. It went so well that Collins hired eight employees and opened the Collins Radio Company.

During World War II, Collins Radio Company supplied radio equipment for the U.S. navy and to England and France, as well. Throughout the war, the company worked night and day, with three shifts of workers. By the 1960s, Collins Radio was one of the largest companies in Iowa. They sold over five hundred radio products and had offices worldwide. In 1965, they estimated that eighty percent of all commercial airlines used Collins equipment. In the 1970s, Collins Radio became part of North American Rockwell Company.

In the 1950s Winnebago Industries started making recreational vehicles at this plant in Forest City when John K. Hansen bought out a small Colorado camper company. Today Winnebago sells thousands of motor homes all over the country.

New businesses in Iowa are not always connected with agriculture, but many are. Sara Lee is one of these companies. In the 1970s, Sara Lee set up a plant at New Hampton where they make cakes, sweet rolls, and frozen dinners. The company decided to locate in Iowa because the state had enough people to work in the plant. The interstate highway system provided good transportation. Most of all, Iowa farms produce the eggs, milk, and meat that are needed for Sara Lee food items.

THE INSURANCE INDUSTRY

The insurance industry has been important in Iowa for over one hundred years. Insurance is a safeguard. In return for regular payments, an insurer agrees to pay the purchaser a sum for loss, damage, or injury. In 1867, Frederick Hubbell started the first insurance company in the state, Equitable Life Insurance Company of Iowa. Hubbell had been buying insurance from an eastern company until he decided to make money by creating his own insurance company.

The second company founded in Iowa was Bankers Life Association. At first the company provided insurance for bankers and their employees but soon it expanded its services. By 1883, Bankers Life was doing business as far away as the state of New York. The company, which has changed its name to the Principal Financial Group, has its headquarters in several large buildings in Des Moines. Today it is one of Iowa's largest private employers, with over four thousand employees. It is the twelfth largest insurer in the United States.

Des Moines is one of the top five insurance centers in the world. Altogether, the Iowa insurance industry employs over sixty thousand people and is still expanding.

Iowans have been making many different products since the state was first settled in the 1830s. In the nineteenth century, industries were mostly related to farming, such as meat packing and breakfast cereals. Today that is still true. The biggest manufacturing business, Deere & Company, employs around ten thousand people in Iowa to make agricultural machinery. The state is trying to encourage other business and industry that are not so closely tied to agriculture, such as the insurance industry. Other examples are high-technology industries using lasers or the latest research in biology.

Iowa is a sensible place for factories to locate because it is near the geographical center of the nation. Products to be sold on either coast do not have to be shipped across the entire country. Today the factories, together with the insurance industry, provide jobs for many Iowans.

FURTHER READING

Bonney, Margaret, ed. "Early Manufacturing." *The Goldfinch* 2, no. 2 (November 1980). Iowa City: State Historical Society of Iowa.

———, ed. "The Town Builders of Iowa. *The Goldfinch* 3, no. 3 (February 1982). Iowa City: State Historical Society of Iowa.

Farley, Mary Allison. "Iowa Women in the Workplace." *The Palimpsest* 67, no. 1 (January/ February 1986). Iowa City: State Historical Society of Iowa.

16 World War I and Hard Times After

In 1914, a terrible war began among the major countries in the world. Although the United States tried to stay out of it, American troops joined the fighting within three years. Once American soldiers were involved, most Iowans strongly supported the war effort. Young men from Iowa farms, small towns, and cities were soon taking their places on the battlefields of France. Farmers back home worked hard to raise more livestock and grow more crops, and Iowa families tried not to waste food and other resources.

When the news of victory finally came, there was wild rejoicing. After the war, however, farmers faced new problems and hard times. They were growing too much food. Prices for their products fell sharply and many had to leave their farms.

THE WAR BEGINS

When Great Britain, France, and Russia joined in a war against Germany and Austria in 1914, all the countries raised huge armies. At the start of the conflict, the United States did not take sides, and President Woodrow

Wilson urged Americans not to do anything that might draw them into the fighting. Some Iowans sent help to homeless European families. Nevertheless, they felt that the causes of the war did not concern this country.

To keep their armies fighting, European countries were willing to pay high prices for food, clothing, guns, and ammunition. American banks even loaned them money to pay for the supplies they bought from the United States. Tons of Iowa corn, pork, and butter were soon sailing across the Atlantic. But selling supplies to Europe created problems for the United States. Neither side in the conflict wanted American supplies to reach its enemies. Great Britain, which had the biggest navy, set up a blockade of ships around German ports and refused to let American ships reach German cities.

In return, the Germans decided to stop supply ships heading to England or France. Because they did not have as many ships as England, they built submarines. A submarine can hide underwater, sneak up on a larger ship, and sink it with a torpedo. German submarines began attacking all ships sailing to England. In 1915, 128 American passengers died when a German submarine attacked and sank the British ship *Lusitania*. The United States demanded an end to submarine attacks. When the Germans refused to stop, the United States declared war on Germany on April 6, 1917, and became a partner of Great Britain, France, and Russia.

SUPPORT FOR THE WAR

The first need was for soldiers because the United States had only a small army. Some men volunteered for the military service, but not nearly enough. The government had to begin to draft soldiers. A law was passed requiring men to serve in the army (or go to prison). Like every other state, Iowa was assigned a certain number of soldiers it had to supply. In each county, all young men had to register with local draft boards. They were each given a number. Then numbers were selected in a drawing by army officials in Washington, and the men in each county who had those numbers were drafted into the army.

Soldiers needed training. In Iowa, the first job was to build army quarters at Camp Dodge, a training camp just north of Des Moines. The first soldiers built dining halls, barracks, and training areas for the troops who would follow. Camp Dodge became the major training center for new Iowa recruits.

The luggage of new recruits at the railroad depot near Camp Dodge during World War I.

The government needed money to pay soldiers and buy supplies. Like other Americans, Iowans bought Liberty Bonds. Each bond was really a loan of money to the government. After the war, the government repaid the bond, plus a small amount extra called "interest." Interest is the price the borrower pays for the use of the lender's money.

Children helped the war effort by buying Thrift Stamps. Post offices sold the 25-cent stamps, which were really small bonds. With the first stamp, the buyer received a card with spaces for sixteen stamps. It cost four dollars to purchase all sixteen stamps. When the card was full, the child paid another twelve cents to register the card in his or her name. The full registered card cost $4.12. In five years, the buyer could take it to the post office and receive five dollars.

In addition to soldiers and money, the war created other needs. The fighting destroyed many homes of European families, and the Red Cross was organized to help the needy. The Red Cross was not run by the government – people donated their time and money to it. This organization built camps to house the homeless, fed the hungry, and moved the injured to safer places.

In Iowa, most towns had a local Red Cross chapter. Women and children made bandages for the wounded or knit sweaters and socks for soldiers, often pinning a cheerful note to them. Sometimes, a local chapter bought sewing machines and set them up at their headquarters. Sewing pajamas and robes for the wounded, women kept the machines busy all day. Iowa Red Cross workers alone made over fifteen million items for soldiers and hospitals.

FOOD PRODUCTION

As the war continued, food became scarce in Europe. Farms became battlefields, and naval blockades prevented supply ships from reaching European ports. The American government printed posters declaring "Food Will Win the War" and promised to pay top prices for the crops farmers grew and for the livestock they took to market.

Iowa has always been a leader in food production,

but during wartime, its farms produced even more. Farmers plowed up grass pastures to plant corn and oats. They raised more cattle and hogs and bought new machinery to do more work. Banks loaned money to help farmers buy what they needed. With the high prices they were getting, farmers thought they could easily pay back the money they borrowed.

Many town families planted large "victory gardens." Canning and preserving their own vegetables, these families had to buy less from stores, which left more food to ship to Europe. To do their part for the war, children often did much of the gardening.

A poster urging farmers to make extra efforts to boost production.

258

Iowa State College at Ames (now Iowa State University) played an important role in boosting food production. It hired experts to study better ways of farming and sent men around the state teaching farmers how to produce even larger crops. An extension agricultural agent in each county passed along information about the most modern ways of farming.

Because of all of these efforts, Iowa food production rose. Iowa farms produced one hundred million more bushels of corn in 1920 than they did in 1917. There were many more cattle and hogs.

At the same time, families learned to use less food. The government rationed (put limits on) how much of certain kinds of food a family could buy. During the war, meat and flour were limited and sugar was rationed to four ounces per day. Families pledged to save food. On Tuesdays, they did not eat meat of any kind, and on Saturdays, they did not eat any pork. Iowans promised to eat no bread or baked goods on Mondays and Wednesdays and only at one meal on other days of the week. Instead of bread, they often ate potatoes, sometimes from their own victory gardens. Most people saw rationing as an important way to help the soldiers.

Because Americans used less and farmers produced more, the United States had food to send to its European partners. When the war left many thousands of European families with little to eat, the American government sent them tons of food. President Wilson chose an Iowan, Herbert Hoover, to take charge of getting this food to those who needed it. During the war, Hoover did an excellent job of running the rationing program. After the war, he turned to the work of feeding hungry European families. Many people were kept from starving, and both Americans and Europeans developed a deep respect for Hoover.

President Herbert Hoover.

As the situation in Europe improved, Hoover came back to work for the government in Washington. In 1928, he was elected President of the United States, the only Iowan ever to hold that office. Today, people visit his birthplace and the presidential library in West Branch.

PROBLEMS AT HOME

The German-Americans

During World War I, many Americans came to dislike Germany very much. They blamed Germany for all the hardship and suffering the war caused. In their anger, many wanted to rid America of anything German. High schools stopped teaching the German language. The governor of Iowa proclaimed that it was against the law

260

to speak foreign languages anywhere in the state. Businesses with German names often chose different ones. Towns like Germania and Berlin dropped their German names. Even in little things, people made changes. Children who got sick with German measles were said to have "liberty measles." Sauerkraut was renamed "liberty cabbage."

However, many Iowa families had immigrated from Germany. Some still spoke the German language and practiced German customs. They had relatives and friends in Germany, and they were proud of their German heritage. While most were loyal to America, they still felt ties to their homeland. Sometimes these German families were treated badly. People accused them of wanting Germany to win the war or of being German spies. As a result, they were sometimes forced to prove their loyalty to the United States. Some were made to kneel and kiss the American flag. Others were forced to march in patriotic parades and to buy war bonds. Children of German immigrants were occasionally mistreated at school. For Iowans who had come from Germany, the war was very painful.

Influenza

In the fall of 1918 Iowans faced a new enemy, an epidemic of influenza, or "flu." Unlike ordinary flu, this disease was extremely serious. Victims were very sick and some even died. By October, there were so many cases that some towns did not allow people to gather in large groups. Churches stopped Sunday services, and theaters closed. Customers in stores were asked to leave as soon as they made their purchases. Schools were closed, and children were told to stay at home and not go to their friends' houses.

Men were dying by the score.... We stacked them up like cordwood at the side of the troop ship. ...to make room for the living.
—World War I veteran (speaking of influenza, Marshalltown, 1988)

261

Nothing helped. By November, even more people were sick. On Thanksgiving Day, one doctor in a small town got calls from fifty-four patients—all new cases of the flu. There was little that doctors could do, but by Christmas the worst seemed to be over. Schools, churches, and theaters opened again. People began to visit in each others' homes. In a few months, there were almost no new cases. During the epidemic, however, nearly eight thousand Iowans died of the flu, almost four times as many as were killed in the war in Europe.

Merle Hay of Glidden, one of the first three American soldiers killed in World War I. After the war, his body was returned to his hometown, where a large stone monument was erected in his memory.

State Historical Society

VICTORY IN EUROPE

On November 11, 1918, Americans heard the news they had been waiting for. The war was over! Germany was defeated, and both sides had signed an armistice (agreement to quit fighting). Celebrations began. Church bells rang, fire sirens sounded in the middle of the night, and people rushed out of their houses to find out what had happened. In many places, there were huge bonfires in parks and public squares. Bands played, and churches held special services to give thanks for victory. November 11 became a national holiday called Armistice Day.

The war was over, but it took months for ships to bring all the men home. Many Iowa soldiers had been killed in the fighting. It could take several weeks to get the news to their families, so some reports that a soldier had been killed arrived after the Armistice celebration. That was sad news indeed. There were 114,224 Iowans who served in the army, navy, or Marine Corps, including 611 nurses. Almost 2,000 were killed in action. Another 1,600 died of sickness or other causes.

PROBLEMS AFTER THE WAR

People were glad the war was over. They wanted things to be normal again, but the war had brought changes and new problems. Farmers in particular were in trouble. While the war lasted, they made more money than ever before. Many wanted bigger farms to increase their production and were willing to pay top prices for land. Even people who did not farm borrowed money from banks to buy farmland and hired someone to farm it for them. As a result, the price of farmland rose rapidly. A typical Iowa farm that cost $20,000 before the war was selling for $40,000 shortly after the war ended.

Soon there was trouble. With peace in Europe, there was not so much need for Iowa farm products. European farms began to grow crops again. Those countries no longer needed to buy grain and meat from America to feed their armies. In spite of that, American farmers continued to produce more and more. With the new machinery they had bought during the war, farmers grew more crops to pay back the money they had borrowed for land and new machines.

By 1920, there was too much grain and livestock. The price for corn, hogs, and cattle fell sharply. In 1920, a bushel of corn sold for $1.19. In 1921, the price was only 41 cents. When farmers got less money for their crops, they could not pay back their loans. Many had to sell their farms to pay their debts. As land prices slumped, it no longer seemed a good time to be farming. Those who had purchased farms when the prices were high were left with land that was worth much less than they had paid for it.

HARD TIMES

Farmers were not the only Iowans with problems. The bankers who had loaned them money were also in trouble. When farmers could not repay their loans, banks lost their money, and many had to close. People who had put money into the banks could not get their savings back. Nearly every town and city in Iowa had at least one bank that went broke, and most had several. Many people lost their savings.

An abandoned bank. The sudden fall in farm prices in 1921 meant that many farmers could not repay their loans, and bank closings were the result.

State Historical Society

Iowa towns depended on the surrounding farms. If the farmers were not making money, they could not buy as much at the stores. When farm prices fell, Iowa towns and cities also suffered. Many Iowans thought that the government ought to help the farmers. But the government refused to buy what farmers produced and sell it to other countries.

Things got even worse. Ten years after the war, a bushel of corn sold for as little as ten cents. Some farmers burned corn in their stoves to keep warm because they had no money to buy coal. More farmers lost their farms.

Some people who could not repay their loans or pay their taxes became desperate. They urged all farmers to join together and promise not to sell any products at such low prices. In some parts of Iowa, farmers even tried to prevent others from selling their products. They set up blockades on country roads and would not let any trucks or wagons with cream, butter, or livestock get into the towns. This did not last long, nor did it help to raise prices.

By the end of the 1920s, many people besides farmers were worried about their jobs. In fact, by the early 1930s, people all over America were having hard

Our daily paper has stopped and we are not renewing it now. As a matter of economy I am resharpening old razor blades.
—Elmer Powers (July 1932)

Angry farmers prevent a truck carrying livestock from getting to market.

State Historical Society

times. A time when stores, farms, and industries are having a hard time making money is called a depression. This was the worst depression the nation had ever had, the Great Depression.

For farming people times were hard from 1921 on, soon after the end of the World War. When the Great Depression started in 1929, things just became worse for farmers. Some of the Depression problems of farmers were different from those of people living in cities. The diary of Elmer Powers tells us about his life on the farm where he lived with his wife and two children. Mr. Powers wrote in his diary every day, and here are some things he wrote between 1931 and 1936.

1931

Wednesday, May 20.
These farm folks in this county are doing quite well in adjusting themselves to the existing times. Driving along the highway, I picked up a young man who said that he was from the east. He described conditions there, as he sees them, and talked about the bitterness of many of those people. He asked about people here and I told him that folks here always have something to eat and also always have our minds and hands busy. Two things that help much to keep people contented.

Tuesday, June 2.
Worked in corn stalk ground, spring plowed. Plenty of trouble with stalks and lots of hard work to do good cultivating. But not a bad job at that. There wasn't any foreman who had to be pleased or to find fault with my work. I know I can still work here tomorrow. The place won't be shut down.

266

1932

Thursday, July 21.	Our daily paper has stopped and we are not renewing it now. As a matter of economy I am resharpening old razor blades and when I shave I use any kind of soap instead of shaving cream. The oats market is a cent lower today.
Monday, September 19.	Everyone is trading now. I did a little today myself, trading sorghum for grapes. . . . But it is the farm women who think out and do things to save money.
Friday, October 14.	. . . One court house is being heated with corn.
Sunday, December 25.	Our family enjoyed a Christmas Dinner with the old folks at their home in the village. No gifts were exchanged by the grown folks. However, the smaller children were well remembered.

[Throughout 1933 conditions did not improve. Toward the end of the year Mr. Powers wrote that he "could see great need for instant action in aiding agriculture."]

1934

Wednesday, May 23.	I spent the forenoon rebuilding an old cultivator. Buying a new one is out of the question. With these crop prospects anyway.
Saturday, June 30.	This afternoon I attended a dispersal sale of a Holstein herd. A neighbor is working thru the system of "going bankrupt" and the sale is one of the results.
Monday, November 12.	Al came to husk this morning and we finished the job at noon. Of all the crops I have gathered, this is the

poorest one. Our cribs are almost empty and almost all of the feeding season is before us. Now I, like many others, must sell or almost give away hogs because I cannot feed them or buy feed for them.

1935

Saturday, February 16. Tonight we went back to our old custom of driving in to the county seat for the evening. We had not been to town on Saturday night for some time. I went to the implement store and found prices of many articles too high. At least I cannot buy them and pay for them.

Monday, April 19. We stopped at the cold storage plant and learned about the new plan of storing our fresh killed meat in our own rented locker.

Thursday, July 9. The earth is dry and hard and many large cracks are appearing in the stubble field. Any tools that I carry on the binder may be dropped down in these cracks. I tied a string on the handle of a 12 in. crescent wrench and lowered it down a crack. I will not mention the distance. Some things are better left unsaid. . . .

Wednesday, October 23. Today two farm ladies were discussing the problem of how best to remove the printed letters from seed sacks that they wished to use in some of their sewing work. On many farms feed sacks are made up into various useful things by the very resourceful farm women.

Wednesday, December 4. I went to town this morning to see the bankers. I will have to sell grain and livestock to pay the mortgage

268

holder, so that I can get the Federal
Loan.

[The weather in 1936 was unusually bad—a bitterly cold winter, followed by a hot, very dry summer.]

1936

Monday,
January 6.

We had another winter day again and here at the place we sold the baler. In some ways I regret to see it go. The money I received for it will be very useful just now in closing up the loan affairs.

Tuesday,
January 14.

I think I finished the loan business today. I got the Federal Land Bank money and it was sent to pay off the old mortgage. All of the people connected with this problem have been very nice. Tomorrow I think I can begin to plan for a new future.

Wednesday,
January 22.

School attendance was as low as the thermometer. Many schools were closed. No mail anywhere today. The bitter cold was very bad for all livestock.

Friday,
April 14.

We began spring plowing today. We will use both the tractor and the horse plows. A good rain is much needed by all growing things.

Saturday,
June 27.

The heat in our corn fields today was very intense. The pastures are rapidly turning a deep burned brown in color.

Sunday,
July 5.

Late this afternoon I borrowed enough iron pipe to reach from the windmill pump to our garden and will pump water on the garden all night. We do not expect to be able to water all of the garden, but may save some of it—the vegetables that will be most useful for canning purposes.

Sunday, July 19.	The greatest corn crop disaster that our country has ever experienced is upon us. It may take some little time for all people to realize this, but all will know as time goes on.
Tuesday, September 15.	Today was a rainy day, all day. It is the first rainy day for months. It was interesting to watch the livestock and the poultry. The younger ones did not seem to know just what the rain was.
Thursday, October 1.	Since our pastures are becoming green again I have been thinking that we should have more young cattle in them. I drove to see the banker and he favored the idea. He suggested that I go out and buy whatever I wanted and come in and we would fix up a loan to cover the purchases.
Friday, October 2.	I drove over to a neighbors this morning and bot a white face calf from him, paying ten dollars for it. I went to another community sale and bot five more calves. I paid $49.50 for these.
Thursday, December 31.	I have written 1936 for the last time and tomorrow a New Year begins. I am facing it knowing there are hardships in the future for farm folks and I hope there will not be too many for us all.

—Elmer G. Powers

THE GOVERNMENT HELPS THE FARMERS

In 1932, the United States elected a new president, Franklin D. Roosevelt. Iowa usually voted for Republicans. But this time Roosevelt, the Democratic candidate, received more votes than President Hoover, a Republican. In the Great Depression, Iowa wanted new leaders.

President Roosevelt asked an Iowan, Henry A. Wallace, to help with farm problems. Wallace understood farming and corn production very well. He was then the editor of a popular magazine for farmers called *Wallace's Farmer.* Wallace believed that the problem was that farmers grew too much—a surplus. Because there was more food than the country needed, the price for farm products was too low. Farmers must grow less, Wallace declared, and he persuaded the government to pay farmers not to grow so much. While some farmers did not like to be told how much they could grow, most welcomed the help from the government. Gradually, prices began to rise and farmers began to make more money. In 1940, Henry Wallace became vice president of the United States.

World War I brought many changes to Iowa. At first, Iowans wanted the United States to keep out of the fighting, but when America declared war on Germany, they worked hard to support the war effort. In the years after the war, Iowa farmers kept on producing more than they ever had. This soon led to problems because they produced so much that prices were too low. Many farmers lost their farms, and workers in town also had a hard time making money.

Iowans discovered that they lived in a larger world than they had once thought. Events thousand of miles away affected their lives. They could no longer care only about what happened in their own town or state. Iowans learned that they were part of a world community.

FURTHER READING

Carter, Merle Wright, and Dean Gabbert. "Hospital Unit R in World War I: Fairfield to France." *The Palimpsest* 67, no. 5 (September/October 1986). Iowa City: State Historical Society of Iowa.

Grant, H. Roger, and L. Edward Purcell, eds. *Years of Struggle: The Farm Diary of Elmer G. Powers, 1931–1936.* Ames: Iowa State University Press, 1976.

Swaim, Ginalie, ed. "Hard Times in Iowa, 1920s and 1930s." *The Goldfinch* 7, no. 4 (April 1986). Iowa City: State Historical Society of Iowa.

17 Depression, Changing Times, and World War II

The years after the First World War were a time when the new mixed with the old. Horse-drawn wagons and shiny automobiles shared the same roads. An Iowan set a speed record in an airplane. Radios brought music and news into homes, and movie theaters spread across the state. In the 1930s, however, the hard times spread beyond farming and times became tough for most people in the nation. It was the Great Depression, when many people were unable to find work and most families had little money.

Meanwhile, a new leader, called Adolph Hitler, had come to power in Germany. He wanted his country to be the most powerful nation on earth. At the same time, Japan built up its military strength in the Far East. Other countries again prepared for war. The United States had become too involved in world affairs to stand apart.

THE GREAT DEPRESSION

Since the end of the war in 1918, factories had been busy producing goods until there were more than people could buy. Prices for factory products began falling.

When factory owners could no longer sell what they made, they no longer needed as many workers. Workers who lost their jobs had no money to buy things from the stores. As a result, the store owners sold less. They, in turn, quit buying things from factories to put on their shelves. The factory owners then laid off still more workers. Before long, the whole country was having hard times – the Great Depression. In most families only the father had a job outside the home, so if the father lost his job, the family had no income. In the Great Depression, many men lost their jobs. Often the only way they could feed their families was to ask the government for relief (help).

Parade of unemployed men.

The Beuscher Family of Dubuque

[The story of the Beuscher family is like that of many Iowa families in the Great Depression. The Beuschers were interviewed to discover how workers "on relief" felt about being helped by the government. This account of that interview was

273

written in 1937, toward the end of the Depression. At home were Mr. Beuscher, 62; Mrs. Beuscher, 60; Paul, 13; Katherine, 17; Jeannette, 19; and Bob, 21. Married and away from home were Charles, 23; Celia, 25; Butch, 26; Eileen, 28; Helen, 30; and Caroline, 32.]

Mr. Beuscher, 62 years old, had been working for 29 years for the Dubuque railroad shops when they closed in 1931. He was . . . unemployed for 4 years. Tall, gangling, weather-beaten, he stoops forward when he talks so that he may follow the conversation with greater ease, for he is more than a little deaf.

Mrs. Beuscher is 2 years younger than her husband. She is the mother of 11 children, but has found time to make dresses and coats and suits, not only for her own family, but also for customers outside the home.

As they "look back on it," Mr. and Mrs. Beuscher scarcely know how they did manage to get along during the time that he had no regular work. The irregular income from Mrs. Beuscher's sewing continued, though she was forced to lower prices until earnings averaged no more than $3 or $4 a week. For a year after Mr. Beuscher lost his job, the family's only cash income was the four hundred seventy-odd dollars obtained from the insurance policies and Mrs. Beuscher's irregular earnings, as contrasted with the predepression regular income of about $130 a month. . . .

Mr. and Mrs. Beuscher agreed that application for relief was a virtual necessity. Mr. Beuscher remembers going down to the courthouse for the first time as the hardest thing he ever had to do in his life; his hand was "on the door-knob five times" before he turned it. The investigation, which the Beuschers recognized as necessary and inevitable, was so prolonged that Mrs. Beuscher "really didn't think" that the family would ever get relief. But finally, after about 2 months, a grocery order of

> . . . earnings averaged no more than $3 or $4 a week.
> —WPA interview (Beuscher family, Dubuque, 1937)

274

$4.50 was granted. Mrs. Beuscher had long before learned to "manage" excellently on little, and though the order was meager, the family "got along" and "always had enough to eat." Mrs. Beuscher believes that investigators "did the best they could"; she resents only their insistence on the disconnection of the telephone, on which she depended for keeping in touch with her customers.

Soon Mr. Beuscher was assigned as a laborer to county relief work, for which he was paid, always in grocery orders, $7.20 a week; this increased amount gave the family a little more leeway. Yet they were still without much cash. The family's garden for which the city furnished some of the seeds and the plot of ground on the city island, added fresh vegetables to the list of staples which alone could be purchased on the grocery orders; there were even some vegetables to be sold from house to house, and Mrs. Beuscher canned a little almost every day, just as the vegetables were ready for use. One summer she put up 500 quarts of vegetables.

State Historical Society

In both town and country, large gardens provided food and income for Iowa families hard hit by the Great Depression.

Although the Beuschers never felt comfortable about receiving relief, it came to be more or less an accepted thing. "You know, you went down to City Hall, and had to wait in line, and you saw all your friends; it was funny in a way, though it was pitiful, too. . . ."

The family received food orders for only a few months, as Mr. Beuscher was soon assigned to the CWA Eagle Point Park project as a laborer, earning 40¢ an hour. Later he worked on the lock and dam project at 50¢ an hour. . . . Although he was glad to be assigned to projects, there was little essential difference in his feelings about direct relief and about "work relief"; he worked hard for his pay, but still felt that he was being "given something." He has heard many times that persons on relief do not want work but he knows . . . that such is not the case except perhaps in a very few instances.

Although Mr. and Mrs. Beuscher "don't say the depression is over yet," times have been better for them since the late fall of 1935, when Mr. Beuscher was called back to his old work at the shops at the old rate of pay. Mr. Beuscher considers this "regular work," and as such, far superior to relief work, especially as he now "feels more independent." Still, it is not as it was in the old days when 1,500 men were employed rebuilding damaged and out-worn cars. Of the 130 men taken back at the shop, only 25 remain at work, which now consists of wrecking instead of reclamation, and no one of the 25 men knows how long his work will last (Works Progress Administration [WPA] interview, completed Dec. 13, 1937).

Because people were desperate for jobs, the national government began to put people to work. The WPA paid people to build roads, parks, public swimming pools, and buildings. WPA workers in Iowa even wrote books, acted in plays, and painted pictures to decorate public buildings. Another new agency, the Civilian Conservation Corps (CCC), hired men between the ages of eighteen and twenty-five to work on the land. In Iowa, these men planted trees and began projects to save the state's precious soil. The CCC fed the men, provided them with work clothes, and gave them a place to sleep. CCC men generally earned $30 each month, most of which they sent home to help their families.

Income and cost of living, 1934–1936

SALARIES PER MONTH		Clothing—Women	
gas station attendent	$130.00	wool coat	$19.00
waitress	$40.00	shoes	$ 1.00
carpenter	$156.00	hat	$ 2.98
schoolteacher		wash dress	39¢
(for 9 months)	$122	silk dress	$ 7.98
auto mechanic	$130		
bookkeeper	$ 65.00	**Toys**	
university professor	$225.00	small car	10¢
highway patrolman	$125.00	stuffed teddy bear	$1.98
painter	$105.00	sled	$6.95
		bicycle	$19.75
PRICES FOR GOODS		Shirley Temple doll	$4.95
Food		doll buggy	$2.95
bread	10¢/loaf		
sugar	5¢/lb.	**Miscellaneous**	
coffee	37¢/lb.	newspaper	3¢
soup	6¢/can	toothpaste	10¢
canned corn	5¢/can	haircut	25¢
butter	26¢/lb.	shoe repair, soles	$1.00
oleo	17¢/lb.	light bulb	20¢
hamburger	8¢/lb.	soap	10¢
bacon	24¢/lb.	lawnmower	$3.50
oranges	12¢/doz.	blanket, part wool	$2.88
		broom	39¢
Clothing—Girls		washing machine	$44.95
dress	$1.00	electric mixer	$11.95
shoes	$1.00	radio	$59.95
fancy dress	$3.00	telephone	$1.75/month
raincoat	98¢	gasoline	24¢/gal.
Clothing—Boys		**Rent**	
dress trousers	$2.98	**(house with hot water and bath)**	
socks	10¢	5 room house	$30–$40
wool sweater	$1.69	4 room house	$25–$30
boots	98¢		
		Used Cars	
Clothing—Men		1933 Chevrolet sedan	$475
work shoes	$1.98	1930 Ford roadster	$100
wool socks	10¢		
dress shirt	98¢		
trousers	$1.00		

Source: *Goldfinch,* Fall 1978, © State Historical Society of Iowa.

Most people did not get aid from the government or take jobs with a government agency. Their regular jobs paid enough for food and clothing, but few families had much money left over after the bills had been paid. For most Iowans, the Great Depression was a time when they had to do without many things they wanted. Those who lived through that experience did not want to repeat it.

To make matters harder, even the Iowa weather was worse than normal. In 1936, there were so many blizzards in the winter that snowplows could not keep the roads open. Farm families were stranded at home days on end and could not get their milk or butter to town. By February, there was more than three feet of snow on the ground, and drifts in some places rose ten or fifteen feet high. Farmers sometimes had to dig tunnels to their barns through the snow.

State Historical Society

Those who experienced the winter of 1936 did not soon forget it.

Even when the snow melted in the spring, the troubles were not over. The summer of 1936 was scorching hot. Almost no rain fell. Crops dried up in the fields, and winds blew up great clouds of dust. In western Iowa, the dust was sometimes so thick that it hid the sun, and it was dark at noon. Dust settled on everything. It was a very hard year.

State Historical Society

Blowing dust became so bad in the summer of 1936 that the Midwest came to be known as the Dust Bowl.

SOCIAL CHANGES

Life was hard, but it was not entirely gloomy during the Depression years. Few people in Iowa had any idea that there would be another war, and in some ways the 1920s and 1930s were a time of beginnings. Iowans saw remarkable changes, for example, in the way people entertained themselves.

Movies

Before 1900, many Iowa towns had "opera houses" where local residents watched plays, comedy acts, and music groups. Actors and musicians traveled from town to town, and famous men and women sometimes gave

279

lectures at the opera house.

After World War I, the new motion pictures became popular, especially with young people, and opera houses became movie theaters. These were the days of silent movies, and the theater hired a piano player to play along with the film. When there was exciting action the piano player played fast; for a sad scene, the player chose slow tunes. If the piano player could not see the screen, it was hard to know when to change. Later, "talkies" came with their own sound and theater piano players were no longer needed.

Before motion pictures became popular, Missouri Valley, like many small towns, had its own opera house where traveling entertainers performed.

GRANT WOOD: IOWA ARTIST

State Historical Society

In 1930, an Iowa artist displayed some paintings at a show in Chicago. In one, he had painted a farmer and his daughter standing in front of their white frame house. The house had a thin, pointed upstairs window, in the Gothic style, and Grant Wood called the painting, "American Gothic."

That painting made Grant Wood famous. It is perhaps the best known of all American paintings. The two people in the picture looked just right to represent the serious and hard-working families of Iowa. In reality, the people in the picture were Grant Wood's dentist in Cedar Rapids and Wood's sister, Nan.

Wood was born on a farm near Anamosa in 1891. As a farm boy, he often made sketches with charcoal from the stove. When his father died, Grant was ten years old. The family moved to Cedar Rapids where he completed high school. Wood, who knew he wanted to be an artist, took summer art classes in Minneapolis and Iowa City and taught art in high school for five years. In 1923, he went to Europe to study painting in Paris. He returned to Iowa, and by the time he died in 1942, Grant Wood was known worldwide.

Wood's most famous paintings were about things he knew best – Iowa farms. One of his best paintings, "Dinner for Threshers," is a picture of the men on a threshing crew sitting down to eat in the middle of the day. One of Wood's favorite subjects was chickens. One time, he was asked to paint a picture of some ladies who thought their families were very important. In the painting, he made them look like chickens by drawing them with long necks and chicken-beak noses. He said that he disliked groups who thought they were better because of who their ancestors were.

Some of Wood's paintings were almost like photographs. In one, for example, he painted an exact copy of a builder's blueprints. At other times, he let his imagination have fun.

Grant Wood became famous for painting what he knew best, scenes from the land he loved, Iowa.

Radio

The radio also became popular after the war. Invented in 1895, the radio was first used to send telegraph messages. Few people dreamed that it could be used for entertainment, until the first regular radio station began in Pittsburgh, Pennsylvania, in 1919. In the same year, the University of Iowa started an early station, WSUI, which is still operating. In 1921, Iowa State University began broadcasting through station WOI. Two years later, WOI broadcast "The Music Shop." This program, which plays classical music, is one of the oldest radio shows in the nation.

State Historical Society

The University of Iowa had one of the earliest radio stations in the nation.

The first private radio station in Iowa was WOC in Davenport, which began in 1922. Its owner, Col. B. J. Palmer, was a leader in the early radio industry. He bought several other stations, including the powerful WHO station in Des Moines. Iowans traveling in surrounding states in 1930 could tune in to WHO and hear familiar shows and news of Iowa.

TRANSPORTATION CHANGES

During World War I, America had depended on the railroads to haul troops, freight, and supplies. Soldiers from all over the country rode trains to the East Coast to get on ships for Europe. Without the trains, it would have taken the United States longer to get soldiers into the fighting. After the war, however, Iowa and the rest of the nation began to depend less on the railroads because other forms of transportation, particularly the automobile, began to carry passengers and freight.

People began driving automobiles on trips. They could go where and when they wanted without waiting for a train. Trucks also competed with trains. As Iowa improved its country roads and it became easier to drive from place to place, trucks hauled livestock, grain, and manufactured goods. For long shipments of heavy freight, trains were still the best transportation. For shorter trips, however, farmers and factory owners began using trucks.

The use of cars, buses, and trucks hurt the railroads. Because train companies did not make as much money, they quit running as many trains and stopped sending trains to the smaller towns. Still, trains remained important. As late as 1950, there was no place in Iowa that was more than twelve miles from a railroad line.

As late as 1950, there was no place in Iowa that was more than twelve miles away from a railroad line.

283

Flying Machines

Airplanes became a new and exciting way to travel. They weren't the first flying machines. In 1783, a giant balloon filled with gas lifted people into the air in Paris, France. Ten years later the first balloon lifted in America, at Philadelphia. At the Iowa State Fair in Muscatine in 1856, a balloon named *Hercules* rose into the air in front of thousands of amazed Iowans. It stayed up for forty-five minutes and floated fifteen miles. In 1906, a huge balloon floated around the dome of the state capitol building in Des Moines. Balloons, however, took a long time to fill. They were very expensive, traveled slowly, and were never a practical way to travel.

A new flying machine appeared in the early twentieth century. In 1903, two brothers in North Carolina, Orville and Wilbur Wright, built and flew the first airplane. It flew by the power of its own motor. Soon, other flyers built their own machines.

Iowans were among these pioneers of the air. In 1914, the U.S. Post Office decided to see if airplanes could carry the mail from one city to another. The first test was a flight from Des Moines to Chicago, and Billy Robinson from Grinnell was selected as the pilot to make that test flight. He set a new speed record, flying faster than eighty miles an hour between the two cities.

Pilots who had landed in Iowa pastures appreciated the new airports.

SOME PROBLEMS

The Ku Klux Klan

People do not always like changes and sometimes become afraid or angry. They may even form groups like the Ku Klux Klan. The Klan was started in the Southern states after the Civil War to keep black people from voting in elections. The Klan believed that America was for certain white people only. Its members did not want blacks to have the rights that white people have.

Ku Klux Klan Kon Klave at Cherokee in September 1924. White robes, masks, the American flag, and burning crosses were present at Klan rallies.

State Historical Society

The Klan never had many members in Iowa, but there were some. In the 1920s, the Klan tried to turn people against Catholics. The leader of the Catholic Church, the Pope, lives in Italy. Therefore, the Klan said, Catholics were loyal to a foreign leader and less loyal to America than other citizens. The Klan also disliked Jews and some immigrants from Europe, saying that they were not good Americans. The organization tried to frighten members of groups it did not like.

The Klan was a secret organization. Members wore long white robes and masks to their meetings, where sometimes they built huge crosses and set them on fire. No one knew how many members it actually had because leaders kept the information secret. It was not a large organization, however. After 1925, it rapidly became smaller. Most Iowans did not like secret groups that tried to frighten others and were glad to see the Klan lose members.

Prohibition

Another problem in the 1920s involved alcohol. In 1919, the United States passed a law against making and selling liquor (alcoholic drinks). All places that sold liquor were closed because it was illegal to buy alcohol anywhere. Not everyone believed that it was a good law. Some felt that each person should decide whether to drink alcohol. Other Iowans liked the law because they felt that drinking caused many problems.

Some people were willing to pay high prices for liquor even if it was against the law. Soon, lawbreakers were making alcohol for sale. There were so many of these "bootleggers" that the police had a hard time stopping them. In towns where people did not like the law, the police often did not even try to make them obey it. One small town in Carroll County, called Templeton, became well known for making alcohol.

In 1933, America changed the law again. Each state was allowed to make its own rules on the sale of alcohol. In Iowa, people could buy liquor, but only from special liquor stores owned by the state. Never again did Iowa try to put a complete stop to the sale of alcohol.

... the manufacture, sale or transportation of intoxicating liquors ... is hereby prohibited.
—Eighteenth Amendment to the Constitution (January 16, 1919)

286

State Historical Society

Because simple homemade equipment was enough to produce bootleg liquor, government law officers could not totally stop its production during Prohibition.

WAR BEGINS

News of disturbing events in other countries began to worry Iowans. After World War I, Germany had many problems. It had lost the war, lost its large army, lost too many jobs, and owed money to other countries. In 1933, a new leader took control. Adolph Hitler promised to make Germany strong again. He built up the army and navy and created a powerful air force. While he created jobs for German workers, Hitler seized great power for himself.

In 1939, Germany attacked the country of Poland, its eastern neighbor. The Poles fought back, and England and France came to the aid of Poland. Russia, now called the Soviet Union, sent soldiers into Poland to fight the Germans. The Second World War had begun.

Japan was an ally (partner) of Germany and also had been preparing for war. Japanese leaders wanted to take over lands in the Far East. They decided to attack the

United States. The American navy kept many of its largest ships at a base in the Hawaiian Islands called Pearl Harbor. On December 7, 1941, Japanese planes made a surprise attack on Pearl Harbor, sinking ships and killing many American soldiers and sailors.

Radios broadcast the shocking news of the Japanese attacks. Years later, most people could still remember what they were doing when they heard the reports. This meant that America could not stay out of the war. The United States prepared to fight Japan, and also Japan's ally, Germany.

Once again, Iowa men and women put on military uniforms. A total of 263,000 Iowans served in the armed forces during World War II. Most were in the army, about one-fourth were in the navy, and a few were in the Marine Corps and Coast Guard.

Many things were like World War I over again. America needed more food, so Iowa farms began growing more crops. Iowans again had to ration sugar, coffee, and meat. Since America was short of gasoline and rubber tires, Iowans limited the use of their automobiles. The war continued until 1945. In May, Germany surrendered.

The war in Europe was over, but Japan continued to fight in the Far East. All through the war, America was working on a secret weapon, the atomic bomb. Scientists at Iowa State University helped enrich the uranium needed for the project. Their work was kept secret. Only a few people knew what the "Manhattan Project" was all about. By the summer of 1945, American scientists finished their secret project. The United States dropped atomic bombs on two Japanese cities, Hiroshima and Nagasaki, which were almost entirely destroyed. Japan surrendered, and World War II was over at last.

War brought sadness to many families. A family from Waterloo suffered the terrible loss of five sons. The Sullivan brothers had joined the navy after Pearl Harbor and asked to serve on the same ship. In 1943, the Japanese sank the ship they were on. Eleanor Roosevelt, the wife of the President, wrote a letter to the boys' parents telling them how sorry she was. After that, the navy did not allow brothers to serve on the same ship.

There were 4,255 Iowans killed in the war and another 8,398 died while they were in service. The official report lists 11,724 Iowans who were wounded in the fighting. Many more would never forget horrible scenes of battle and suffering.

The twenty years between the two world wars saw many kinds of change in Iowa. For most farmers, these were hard years. Prices for crops were so low that many farmers lost their land and had to leave their farms. The Great Depression also made life hard in the city. Factory workers who lost their jobs had little money to live on. Yet life in Iowa had improved in some ways. Radio and the movies were new forms of entertainment. People with cars could travel more easily.

The war brought an end to the Depression by creating jobs. America needed all the food that farmers could grow, and farm prices increased. Iowans served in the American armed forces and fought battles all over the world. Many were injured and some were killed.

Iowans wondered what their future would be after the war. Would there be another depression? Could nations learn to live together in peace? What would life be like on the farms and in the towns and cities? Would there be even greater changes in the years ahead?

> **Older men declare war. But it is youth that must fight and die.**
> —Herbert Hoover (1944)

FURTHER READING

Bonney, Margaret, ed. "War!" *The Goldfinch* 4, no. 4 (April 1983). Iowa City: State Historical Society of Iowa.

"The Depression and After." *The Palimpsest* 63, no. 1 (January/February 1982). Iowa City: State Historical Society of Iowa.

"The Great Depression." *The Goldfinch* (Fall 1978). Iowa City: State Historical Society of Iowa.

Meusburger, Joanne. "Farm Girl." *The Palimpsest* 68, no. 4 (Winter 1987). Iowa City: State Historical Society of Iowa.

Saloutos, Theodore, and John D. Hicks. "The Farm Strike." In *Patterns and Perspectives in Iowa History,* Dorothy Schwieder, ed. Ames: Iowa State University Press, 1973.

"Some Thoughts on Prisoners of War in Iowa, 1943 to 1946." *The Palimpsest* 65, no. 2 (March/April 1984). Iowa City: State Historical Society of Iowa.

18 The Story Continues

The years since World War II have been important ones for Iowans. New inventions such as television, jet airplanes, and computers have changed the way they live. Many more young people are going to college. Small farms have been combined to form bigger ones. Fewer farm families work the land, rural schools have fewer students, and stores in small towns serve fewer people. At the same time, Iowans have become more involved in world events. Today, Iowa products are sold all over the world, Iowans travel more, and television and radio keep Iowans informed of national and world-wide events that will affect their lives.

Iowans have had to adjust to these changes and to learn new ways of doing things. They try to save the best from the past while they add the advantages of the present.

FARMING AND RURAL LIFE

In Iowa, the population of rural areas has been falling for the past hundred years. Many counties had more people in 1900 than they have today. Where four or five families once lived on a square mile of farmland, today there may be only two or three. Those who still live on the farm usually work more land. The size of farms is measured in acres. In 1950 an average farm was 170 acres. In 1982, the average was 280 acres. By 1986, the average farm was 308 acres.

Larger farms means fewer farms. Bigger tractors and machinery help farmers to farm more land and do work that once was done by people. Because fewer people are needed to farm, many families get jobs doing something else. In 1950 there were 200,000 farms in Iowa. In 1982 there were 115,000. By 1986, there were only 109,000 farms.

Iowa farmland values

Year	Cost per Acre
1900	$ 43
1910	96
1920	255
1930	135
1940	84
1950	197
1960	237
1970	385
1975	719
1980	1811
1985	1065

State Historical Society

Modern machinery can finish in a few hours the plowing that took pioneer farmers several days.

This change has brought problems to rural areas. Some schools have closed and sent students to a neighboring town. Stores have gone out of business because there were not enough customers. Doctors are hard to find because they would rather work in larger towns where hospitals have better equipment. Still, families on farms and in small towns usually like their communities and want to stay where they are. Many towns try to create new jobs to keep people there.

A smaller farm population has brought another change. Legislators, who make laws for the state, are elected to represent a certain number of voters. When more people lived on farms, most legislators came from rural areas. The laws they passed were often to help farmers. Since World War II, fewer legislators have come from rural areas and more have come from the cities. For farmers, this means that the laws may be what city people want rather than what farmers want.

Even though there are fewer farm families, Iowa farms produce more than ever before. The total sales from all the products grown in Iowa in 1986 came to nine billion dollars. In 1985 the United States sold forty-five million tons of corn and seventeen million tons of soybeans to foreign countries. Iowa was a leading state in growing both of these crops. Because Iowa sells so much overseas, what happens all over the world affects Iowa. For example, when a long dry spell in Brazil hurt that country's soybean crop, the price for Iowa soybeans went up. Iowa is indeed part of a world market.

Iowa farmers have learned how to produce large harvests, but producing too much can be a problem. Prices are kept low when farmers produce too much. In the 1950s, the U.S. government started a Soil Bank program to help farmers. Farmers were paid *not* to plant crops in some of their fields. Instead, they planted grasses or other plants to enrich the soil and keep it from eroding (washing away). The Soil Bank lasted only a few years because the government decided it cost too much money. However, it made people aware that Iowa was losing its most important resource—valuable topsoil. On October 4, 1979, Pope John Paul II came to Iowa. Speaking to 340,000 people gathered at Living History Farms in Des Moines, he declared that the rich Iowa soil "must be preserved with care, for your children and your children's children."

© 1985: The Des Moines Register and Tribune Company; reprinted with permission

Brian Duffy's cartoon points out the worldwide problem of soil erosion. Iowa has lost half of its fertile topsoil since pioneers first plowed the prairie.

Iowa has produced some of the world's experts on farming, people who have discovered new ways to grow food. One is Dr. Norman Borlaug, who was born on a farm near Cresco in Howard County. He helped to develop new varieties of wheat that produce more grain.

The new wheat is grown in countries where people desperately needed more food. As a result of his work, Dr. Borlaug was awarded the Nobel Peace Prize in 1970. He was the first plant scientist ever to receive the famous award, which is given to people who make the world a better place.

Plowing that follows the contour of the land helps to keep Iowa's valuable soil from washing away.

State Historical Society

CHANGES IN EDUCATION

School Consolidation

Because fewer people live in the country, there are fewer children in rural schools. In the 1950s some high schools had fewer than ten students in a grade. School officials argued that it was hard to give students in smaller schools the same opportunities as students in larger schools. Teachers in small schools had to teach several subjects. It was too expensive to provide good libraries and special science equipment, and there were fewer students for sports and music activities.

294

In the 1950s, small schools began to consolidate. Small towns combined schools or sent their students to larger towns nearby. Good roads and buses made it easier to send children farther to school. In 1953, there were 4,558 school districts in the state. In 1960, the number had fallen to 1,575 districts, and by 1985, there were only 438.

Many people in smaller towns were sorry to see their schools close and disliked busing their children to schools many miles away. They also missed the local school sports, music events, and plays. Others were glad that their children could attend bigger schools because they believed that the children would get a better education.

Colleges and Universities

There were other changes in education. When Iowa was first a state, college was only for the wealthy. In the 1960s, more students began attending college. The government offered to lend money to students who paid back the loans when they got jobs after college. In Iowa and across the nation, colleges and universities grew rapidly. They needed to hire more teachers and build more dormitories where the students could live. In 1960, the three Iowa public universities—the University of Iowa, Iowa State University, and the University of Northern Iowa—had 24,000 students. In 1970, they were teaching 52,000 students. By 1985 there were 68,000 students in these three schools.

Other students were taking different kinds of classes after high school. In 1965, Iowa created fifteen vocational schools around the state where students learn the skills to do a job or trade. Some learn how to fix cars, while others learn how to be carpenters, chefs, bricklayers, or secretaries.

In 1985, there were over 150,000 students in Iowa universities, vocational schools, and private colleges. Nearly one person out of every twenty Iowans was taking some college courses that year.

NEW DIRECTIONS

Television

At 6:30 in the evening on February 21, 1950, something new was in the air—an Iowa television broadcast. It was coming from station WOI-TV in Ames. For several years, WOI was the only television station in central

VIETNAM WAR PROTESTS

In the 1960s, the United States sent soldiers to fight in southeast Asia. Soon, thousands of soldiers were fighting in the jungles of Vietnam. Many Americans objected to sending U.S. soldiers to fight in an Asian war and wanted the United States to bring its soldiers home.

There was soon trouble at many colleges. Students disliked the war and did not want to become soldiers in it. To try to stop the fighting, they held public meetings to protest what the government was doing. Sometimes they sat down in the middle of highways and refused to let cars and trucks pass. Sometimes they took over college buildings or blocked doorways to classes. Police arrested some students and put them in jail. In 1970, when student protests against the war were at their peak, many colleges dismissed classes early in the spring, sending students home to keep the unrest from getting worse. Only when the war in Vietnam was over did colleges return to normal.

Iowa, and for a while Channel 5 was the only channel to watch. Television quickly became very popular. Many families bought television sets in the early 1950s, and TV performers were known wherever they went.

For generations farm families had been used to coming into town on Saturday night to do their shopping. While the children went to the movies, adults visited with friends. Stores stayed open until midnight. When television came, however, families hurried home to watch their favorite shows. Store owners in one town remember how people began leaving town to be home by 9:00 P.M. in time for Saturday night wrestling, a very popular show in the early days of television. After that,

Students at the University of Iowa demonstrate their opposition to the Vietnam War.

spending Saturday night in town was never as popular as it once had been.

The television set became a familiar feature in Iowa living rooms in the early 1950s.

Travel

New developments in transportation helped Iowans travel faster and faster. In 1956, the United States began building interstate highways to connect major cities. Cars and trucks could travel from one coast to the other without ever stopping for a stop sign.

Iowans also began traveling more by air. By 1950, there were 6,000 pilots in Iowa and over two hundred airports. Some airports could only handle small planes. City airports, however, were busy with planes flying in from all over the nation. Airline companies had flights on a regular schedule, and Iowans could buy an airline ticket as easily as they once bought a train ticket. Iowans could be in distant cities within a few hours, trips that had taken their grandparents days or even weeks to make. This was another way in which Iowa was truly becoming part of a world community.

But with all the new forms of transportation, Iowans have not forgotten bicycles. Every summer, thousands of Iowans take part in a bicycle ride across the state, sponsored by the *Des Moines Register.* RAGBRAI (the *Register's* Annual Great Bicycle Ride Across Iowa) winds through the Iowa countryside in late summer. It starts somewhere along the Missouri River in the west and ends as bikers reach the Mississippi.

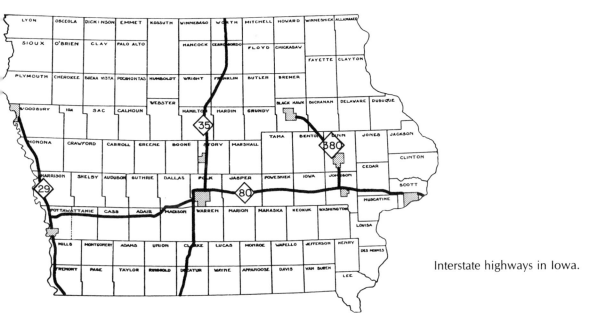

Interstate highways in Iowa.

Outer Space

Some Iowans were even taking an interest in outer space. Dr. James Van Allen, an astronomer at the University of Iowa studying the stars and planets, discovered some new facts about the layers of air surrounding the earth. The University of Iowa has made parts for rockets sent into space, and Iowa scientists helped to make satellites that circled the earth. Discovering new things about the universe we live in, Dr. Van Allen and other Iowa scientists have helped put Americans into space.

UPS AND DOWNS FOR IOWANS

In the 1980s, the Iowa economy went through hard times. After the high prices for crops in the 1970s, there was a sudden drop in prices. Many farmers who had borrowed money to buy land or equipment could not pay back their loans. They lost their farms and had to find other jobs. If they could not find jobs in Iowa, they had to move out of the state. Some factories that made farm machinery closed, and those workers had to look for new jobs. Many towns and cities lost population during the 1980s.

The government began to try to bring new industries to Iowa. They wanted businesses to open factories that would create jobs for Iowans. By the end of the 1980s, things were better but Iowa farms and businesses still had not achieved the success they had known in the 1970s. Losing population continued to be a problem.

The story of Iowa includes the story of the land, rivers and streams, homes, schools, towns, farms, stores, pigs, cattle, chickens, horses, buggies, cars, jets, computers, and the people – old and young, men and women. Each person who has lived here has played a part.

And the story is not finished. It continues every day as people work and play. The first American Indians who hunted large animals along Iowa's rivers would have found the cabins of the pioneers very strange. They would have marveled at the iron pots on the fireplaces and the glass in the windows. The pioneers would find the homes of today with their microwave ovens and television equally strange.

We do not know what homes and schools a hundred years from now will be like, but we know that they will be different from our own. What new inventions will there be? What will happen to the land? Will the weather be the same as it is now? What crops will we grow?

Learning about the past helps us realize that we all play a part in history. We have inherited communities, inventions, and ideas from those who have lived before us. What we do with what we have affects all of us now and those who will come after us. There are millions of characters in the Iowa story—Black Hawk, Annie Wittenmyer, Carrie Chapman Catt, Herbert Hoover, James Van Allen, and you.

Iowa rolls onward with the rolling world, A place of trust in a time not to be trusted.
—Paul Engle (Iowa poet, "Heartland," 1977)

FURTHER READING

Boyle, Matthew. "Serving the Cause of Peace: The Iowa Campuses' Vietnam Protest." *The Palimpsest* 63, no. 5 (September/October 1982). Iowa City: State Historical Society of Iowa.

Smith, Thomas S. "The Vietnam Era in Iowa Politics." *The Palimpsest* 63, no. 5 (September/October 1982). Iowa City: State Historical Society of Iowa.

Warren, Wilson J. " 'The People's Century' in Iowa: Coalition-Building among Farm and Labor Organizations, 1945–1950." *The Palimpsest* 49, no. 5 (Summer 1988). Iowa City: State Historical Society of Iowa.

Index

305